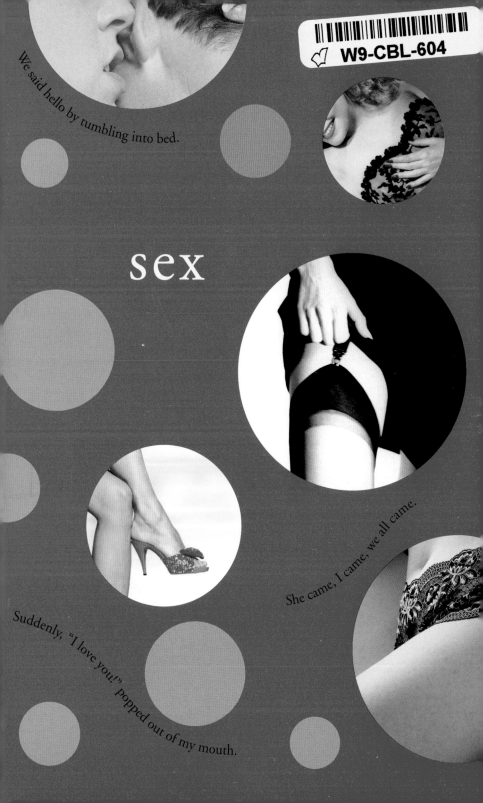

We said hello by tumbling into bed.

sex

She came, I came, we all came.

Suddenly, "I love you!" popped out of my mouth.

sex
and
sensibility

sex
and
sensibility

∼ 28 True Romances
from the Lives of Single Women

edited by GENEVIEVE FIELD

WASHINGTON SQUARE PRESS
New York   London   Toronto   Sydney

WSP

Washington Square Press
1230 Avenue of the Americas
New York, NY 10020

Library of Congress Cataloging-in-Publication Data

Sex and sensibility: 28 true romances from the lives of single women/edited by
Genevieve Field.—1st Washington Square Press trade pbk. ed.
  p. cm.
ISBN 0-7434-8303-0
1. Single women—Biography. 2. Single women—Sexual behavior.
3. Man-woman relationships. I. Field, Genevieve.

HQ800.2.S49 2005
306.7'082'0973—dc22   2004062297

First Washington Square Press trade paperback edition February 2005

10 9 8 7 6 5 4 3 2 1

WASHINGTON SQUARE PRESS and colophon are
registered trademarks of Simon & Schuster, Inc.

For information regarding special discounts for bulk purchases,
please contact Simon & Schuster Special Sales at 1-800-456-6798
or business@simonandschuster.com

Designed by Jaime Putorti

Manufactured in the United States of America

To single girls past, present, and future,
for keeping the faith.

contents

Introduction   xi

STRUMPETS AND RAKES
Confessions of a Teenage Cocktease
   Elissa Schappell   3

Two Dollars a Word
   Precious Williams   15

In the Bowl of Lights That Is La Paz
   Pam Houston   26

Sexual Healing
   Daisy Garnett   32

A Model Boyfriend
   Melissa de la Cruz   47

Suddenly Single
   Liz Welch   57

PARLORS AND PORTS
Travel Love
   Amy Sohn   69

In Translation
   Julianna Baggott   76

How to Be Alone
Lisa Gabriele   86

Around the World in 80 Dates
Susan Dominus   97

Herland, Revisited
Meghan Daum   104

ALLIES AND ENEMIES
Medusa's Sister
Merrill Markoe   115

Do You Take This Woman?
Em and Lo   127

Penelope
Erika Krouse   142

The Feast of San Gennaro
Jennifer Weiner   152

One Way to Stay Warm in Winter
Thisbe Nissen   162

Where the Boys Were
Lily Burana   177

DIVISIONS AND DISPARITIES
Whereya Headed?
Jennifer Baumgardner   189

The So-called Wife
Amy Keyishian   197

Plot vs. Character
Quinn Dalton   206

My Year of Missed Connections
  Mikki Halpin   215

Hiding the Kid
  Lisa Carver   223

ARDOR AND ACHE
Everything I Need to Know about Romance I Learned
from Jane Austen (I Just Wish I'd Taken Her Advice
Sooner)
  Darcy Cosper   233

Cut and Shave
  Laurie Notaro   243

Girl Times Two Minus One
  Rachel Mattson   252

Someone Old, Someone Blue
  Lynn Harris   259

Girl Saves Own Life over Worthless Jerk
  Heather White   264

Waiting
  Eliza Minot   273

Contributor Biographies   277

Acknowledgments   287

introduction

It was two hundred years ago that Jane Austen (just barely out of her teens) began writing *Sense and Sensibility*, a tale of young women in hot pursuit of worthy husbands. That now-classic novel keenly and acerbically portrays a time in which women's fates were inextricably tied to their states of romantic attachment. In those days, of course, single girls with no inheritances had little control over their own destinies, and, it would seem, only their needlepoint and each other's companionship to distract them from thoughts of their marriageability. Tragic existences, indeed! Of course, it would seem that *today's* women are in a completely different place. We have the self-confidence and the carte blanche to put ourselves first, to spend our days competing for jobs with the very same men we might go to bed with at night, to proclaim that marriage is an option but not a holy grail. And our worlds are far less likely than an unlucky Austen character's to come crashing down all around us if we should slip up and let good sex trump good sense.

But in our hearts, are we really such different creatures today? The sometimes troubling truth is that our biological hardwiring hasn't yet caught up to all of this social liberation.

We are still female Homo sapiens, after all, and because we are staying single longer than any generation before us,[1] our sexual independence is often pitted against more prosaic needs.

Ah, those inescapable needs: the nesting urges that—by the time we reach thirty or so—can no longer be satisfied by futon-shopping with our roommates or letting the laundry pile up cozily in our tiny studio apartments; the cravings for intimacy that we try to drown out with loud music and ten-dollar cocktails; and that damning tendency to unzip our hearts along with our pants (for all our bravado, *some* of us have not yet grasped Erica Jong's much celebrated concept of the zipless fuck). The little, yet unmistakable, voice that whispers, "Find the one. Find the one ..." can sometimes put the kibosh on our exhilarated twenty-first–century libidos. Is it so bad to want to be truly taken care of? The answer changes as often as outfits before a first date. But it's that constant push-pull between a single woman's independence and vulnerability, her fearlessness and self-doubt, her inner Mae West (overtly sexual) and her inner Jane Austen (covertly sexual), that makes her an irresistible heroine.

There are multiple heroines in *Sex and Sensibility: 28 True Romances from the Lives of Single Women.* They are the contributors, whose narratives comprise a revealing, funny, sexy manual on the art (and occasional artlessness) of living single. Most of these writers tell their stories not to cru-

---

1. Today, approximately 32 percent of American women betweem the ages of 20 and 44 have never been married, as opposed to 19 percent of women in the same age group in 1970. In New York City, over 40 percent of all adult women have never been married (U.S. Census Bureau).

sade for the single lifestyle but to write about the very part of them that is completely their own—in debauchery, in solitude, in anticipation, in desperation, in lovesickness, and in love. They have much to say about the near-insanity of the dating world. But mostly they just want to tell their best stories—the juicy ones they share with their friends on all those foggy-headed, flushed day-afters. Sometimes, after all, it can be more fun to recount one's dating adventures than to actually live through the dates.

Sex and Sensibility is divided into five parts, each about a different aspect of being single. In Strumpets and Rakes writers dish about the bad boys they've fallen for and about being bad themselves—and the stories are especially sexy. Elissa Schappell plays the field, disengaging herself from her sexual conquests until she meets the man she'll either have to "marry or kill" because no one else must have him; Precious Williams, a music journalist, fesses up to her penchant for male rap stars and the lengths to which she'll go to get their stories; Pam Houston naïvely follows a dashing stranger up to his penthouse while on a writing assignment in Bolivia; Daisy Garnett unwittingly prostitutes herself to write a story about a rogue sexual healer for a glossy magazine; Melissa de la Cruz remembers her sexual infatuation with a male model and the little white lies she told to convince him of her worthiness; and finally, Liz Welch dodges a bullet when she escapes her engagement to a preppy rogue.

Parlors and Ports is about feeling set off from the world— alone, but not necessarily lonely. Amy Sohn opens this chapter with a sweet tale of anticipation over a visit to the guy who might be the One; Julianna Baggott reminisces about her tumultuous college love affair with a brooding Frenchman; Lisa Gabriele admits that her penchant for long-distance relationships is her excuse for living the way she lives best—alone; Susan Dominus writes about exercising her travel lust through a series of international lovers; and Meghan Daum muses on how the legendary "man shortage" in New York City made her a better woman.

In Allies and Enemies, writers pay tribute to the friends who've helped them through hard times, the competitors who've stolen their men, and the lovers who've turned out to be enemies. Merrill Markoe shocks with a devastating and yet darkly hilarious tale of the summer in college when she both lost her virginity and was raped; the literary duo Em and Lo muse that their intense friendship will probably be the closest thing to marriage they ever find; Erika Krouse recounts a dear friend's long overdue escape from the grips of a cheating boyfriend; Jennifer Weiner seeks relief from dieting in a sexual encounter. Thisbe Nissen finds temporary security in a threesome; and Lily Burana describes how being an outcast in high school drove her straight into the arms of the gay male community, where she learned how to love.

Divisions and Disparities is about wanting what we can't have, making bad choices, and feeling that happiness and romance, which our friends seem to find so easily, will always elude us. Jennifer Baumgardner tries to understand why she can have orgasms with women but not with men; Amy Keyishian realizes she's made the biggest mistake of her life by getting married; Quinn Dalton describes a film school love affair that taught her—the hard way—to distinguish between real-life relationships and movie romances; Mikki Halpin turns to cyberspace to find the soul mate she keeps missing in real life; and single mom Lisa Carver tries unsuccessfully to hide the fact of her motherhood from her new lover.

In Ardor and Ache, about the quest for the loves of our lives, Darcy Cosper outlines the dating wisdom she learned from reading Jane Austen; Laurie Notaro relates a hilarious, if humiliating, series of attempts to bed her secret crush; Rachel Mattson, a privileged Jewish daughter, gets her heart broken by a beautiful Puerto Rican girl; Lynn Harris bemoans that she's always a bridesmaid (or at least a wedding guest) but never a bride; Heather White splits with her drug-addicted fiancé and flees to New York City to find herself and rejuvenate her sex life; and Eliza Minot pays poetic tribute to the endless cycle of "tiptoe[ing] around the edges of intimacy, avoiding yourself, trying to be yourself, having sex, leaving people, being left" that is single life.

And me? Why am *I* presenting these modern-day love and lust stories? First, a confession: I'm married. I have no plans to get unmarried, ever. But I will probably always write about the time I was single and remember the powerful ambivalence I felt about dating. While I craved the attention, companionship, and sex that came with it, I was often saddened by the fleetingness of the connections I made with men in those days. And now, as I read and reread this roller-coaster collection of confessions about new connections, new sex, new love, new loss, I find myself thinking, Wow, I'll never feel those things again—and then, Whoa, I'm feeling them *now*. They're all here, inside these two covers, just waiting to be rediscovered.

—Genevieve Field

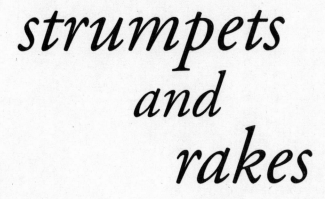

strumpets
and
rakes

confessions of a
teenage cocktease ·

ᴄ᷎ elissa schappell

I blame the suburbs for making me a cocktease. Growing up
in a small town in Delaware there were no malls, movie
theaters, or cafés within walking or biking distance. There
were no museums, no galleries, no book or record stores.
There were, however—in abundance—boys.

Thus, my girlfriends and I spent a lot of restless hours
hanging out at each other's houses, lying on canopy beds or on
the shag-carpeted floor, door locked, tickling each other's
arms and backs, gossiping about boys and what we'd do with
one if we ever got one, occasionally hopping off the bed to
dance in front of the mirror, lip-synching Cheap Trick's "Sur-
render" into a hairbrush. In the summer we went to the

neighborhood pool and tanned on top of picnic tables, running across the hot macadam parking lot in bare feet when we heard the ice cream truck, or we biked to a swimming hole with a rope swing off a bridge, occasionally flashing motorists.

At night we prowled in darkness, rearranging the letters on people's mailboxes to spell curse words, or we amused ourselves by putting one neighbor's lawn furniture in his next door neighbor's car. Tired of petty vandalism, we hung out in each other's driveways, or on occasion headed over to somebody's house, and down into a finished basement or den to watch the neighbor boys shoot pool or play foosball, The Beach Boys, Bruce Springsteen, or maybe The Clash on the stereo.

On some evenings (maybe it had to do with the phases of the moon) a sort of erotic terminal velocity would be reached and someone would suggest putting on something slower, like Led Zeppelin, and pairing up. This was offered in the same way that, had it been all girls, someone might have said, "Hey, let's have a séance," or "Who wants to play Light as a Feather?"

These weren't make-out parties like people would later have in high school, where couples slipped off into bedrooms and linen closets. These were unchoreographed, purely spontaneous eruptions of adolescent lust. Always there was this sinking feeling in the pit of my stomach as I did the math—was there a girl for every boy? In those awkward moments of sussing out the numbers, it almost seemed as though my peers were magnetized, drawn inexorably to each other by complementary charges, as I ricocheted back and away into a corner. (Admittedly, coupling up wasn't quite as excruciating as picking teams in gym class, where me and the girl in the helmet were always the last two standing. The phrase "You get Schappell" haunts me still.)

So what to do? Should I make an excuse—headache, curfew—and beat a hasty retreat home? Being the extra girl (the extra boy generally sat and watched) meant being exiled to TV upstairs with the younger siblings and unsuspecting parents: pure torture. It had happened to me once, and as I'd trudged numbly up the stairs, blind with humiliation, I'd sworn I would never let it happen again.

The ritual dictated that girls sat in the boys' laps or beside them, and you made out for the length of a song. When it ended you rose and moved on, a perfect circuit of blue-eyed geisha girls in cutoffs. Sometimes, if the song was going on too long or they were desperate to hook up with the next person in line, someone would yell out, "Switch."

Although I lived in fear of someone yelling out "Switch" on me, it was still heaven.

Nobody got hurt, and nobody got bored; the worst thing to happen was a cold sore. In this way I learned how to kiss, learned each boy's kiss was as distinctive as his laugh. Some kissed with their teeth, some slobbered, some chewed on your lips like taffy, and others could kiss in a way that made you feel like your blood had been turned to butter. I could have identified those teenage boys in the dark by kiss alone. When it was over, only when I'd tempted breaking curfew or missing dinner, I'd leave with a girlfriend, the two of us sprinting away from the house, sneakers pounding through backyards, laughing, reeling, and drunk on hormones—something *real* had just happened to us. Free from any uncomfortable small talk, any kiss-or-no-kiss-at-the-door awkwardness, we were nothing but desired. It never occurred to me that boys were about as sexually discerning as farm animals.

Sometime around seventh grade, it was officially ordained that I was not really girlfriend material. Sure I had a nice rack, long blondish-brown hair, and didn't seem too smart despite my glasses (I'd learned early that boys liked dumb girls best), but, sadly, as one of my friend's mothers had put it, I just wasn't right in the head.

At that age it wasn't obvious in pictures; there was no punk rock dye job, no nose ring. It was easy to wear the right clothes, the grosgrain headband, the madras pants and Fair Isle sweaters, tennis skirts and docksiders. It was easy to outwardly assimilate, but my inside? That I couldn't fake. As soon as I opened my mouth I was revealed. Unfortunately I talked all the time. I cracked wise, I did imitations, I asked dumb questions like, If you had to sacrifice one of your senses, what would it be, and why? Or, Let's say that a starving man steals a loaf of bread to feed his wife and children, is that really stealing? Questions that had people shaking their heads. "You are so strange," they'd say. "Cute, but strange."

Thus, every night after asking God to bless the souls of my dead grandparents, and to let me die before my parents did, as I could not live without them, I'd add, *and please God just make me normal, don't let me be a nymphomaniac, or a lesbian like those girls on the volleyball team—even though they seem really happy.* . . .

I was worried about my sexual curiosity—my desire to binge at the banquet of teenage carnality. Was it so wrong to want to know if it felt the same way with this one as it had with that one? If I started having sex, would I ever be able to stop? Was having sex like peanuts and tattoos—you couldn't have just one?

Things changed in high school once kids started getting their licenses. The stakes got higher, and more interesting. It wasn't uncommon, at the end of a double-date, to end up parking in a field or an empty lot. While one couple made out in the backseat, the other went at it in the front. It all felt very thrilling and wrong, and terribly sexy.

The trick was you and your girlfriend had to decide ahead of time how far each of you was going to go, otherwise it became a competition—he has her shirt off, and your boyfriend doesn't have yours. Of course once the windows began to fog up and everyone was stupid with lust, all bets were off. Inevitably, my date and I would be the ones booted out of the car—first undressed got dibs on the wagon.

I wasn't going to get even a little nude, because no matter how many tequila sunrises I drank, how much hash-under-glass was enjoyed, I wasn't going to seriously fool around in a car with another couple. No way. Not the first time, and probably not ever. Witnesses? Are you joking? Once you had sex it was all over. Your passport got stamped HUSSY and there was no return. If you slept with a boy it was either because you two were serious, very serious, or you were a slut. I knew, deep, deep, down inside me, that no boy in this town was ever going to be in love with me, or me in love with him. I also knew that this made me different from other girls, and different was bad. Different could, no matter what you did, get you a bad reputation.

The only solution was to keep moving along, smiling, remembering what my mother once told me (she herself was a spirited, fun-loving lass, as was my grandmother): *Be a good date, not a great date, a good date.* I read this as: *Don't flirt with his friends, don't leave with someone else (you've got to dance with those that brung you), and don't go all the way.* Going all the way was pretty much like just throwing up your arms and saying, "Game over." I didn't want to go all the way. All I really wanted was to have some fun. I liked chasing boys, hooking them, and reeling them in. Getting my picture taken with my trophies, and then letting them go. When they said, "I'll call you," my heart pounded simultaneously with, *Oh please do*, and, *Oh please don't.*

I knew it would only be a matter of time before they saw my true colors: before I would burst into tears at seeing a Christmas tree put out for the trash, or jump out of the car at a red light in an unspeakable fury of some sort; before my insistence on kissing endlessly, and the matter of my not going all the way, would become an issue; before curiosity would kill the cat, and I'd start thinking his best friend was cuter, more interesting, more unknowable than he was, and wanting him.

I knew it was just a matter of time before we'd be ignoring each other in the hallways, and my friends would be shaking their heads at my cupidity, and his friends would be sniggering, and saying mean things, running me down, and I'd feel like a fool, and I'd be so, so angry. Why, oh why, couldn't I be a boy? I would wonder. Why couldn't I be some charming cad, a Casanova, instead of a holding-tight-at-second-base slattern?

Not long ago I sought out some old diaries of mine. Flipping through them, I searched for the early roots of depression, glimmers of nascent genius; instead what I found were the rantings of a horny Pollyanna afflicted with Attention Deficit Disorder.

It's over with Craig, I have been crying for hours. Last Friday I made out with Joey at the Tower Hill dance, he is such a good kisser! He says he doesn't like Missy any more. God! Of course Chris was mad when he saw me with him. He tells me he wants to do things to my body, things that I'd like. I think I could love him. I wish he wasn't drunk so much. Oh well! Maybe I still like Chris. What is wrong with me? I don't know! I am so confused, and I am hurt too. Also, then there's Phil. I think I could really like him. . . .

Good God. Someone should have turned a fire hose on me.

Before I set off for college, my doctor gave me a prescription for birth control pills.

"If I had a daughter that looked like that," he said to my mother, "I'd put her on the pill."

It is hard to say who was more horrified by this statement, me or my mother. Let's call it even. I had no intention of having sex any time soon. After all, my mother had insisted that sex really wasn't good unless it was with someone you loved, and I believed her. I hadn't really loved anyone, I had been made dizzily happy and alternately miserable by boys. Tortured with longing, yes, but loved?

Perhaps it was in part my father's fault. My father had always told me the boys in my world weren't worth my pining away for. He even warned me: *Never overestimate a boy's intelligence or his honesty.* In other words, sex with a dumb, lying bastard was probably going to be pretty lousy. I would come to find out, in college, that this wasn't exactly true.

In college, emboldened by drink and a Holly Golightly complex, I grabbed boys and kissed them in the street. It was a thrill, a rush. Wasn't anything possible in a world where people just embraced on the street then moved on? Wasn't life just grand? Why shouldn't life be a big box of chocolates, and all the boys caramel creams? Just one sweet crush after another.

By my sophomore year, when the song "Runaround Sue" came on at parties, my friends would scream my name and dance around me in a circle. They joked that on my wedding day I'd still be trying to choose which groom to walk down the aisle with.

"Walk?" I'd say. "Honey, by the time I am ready to settle down, I will be in an iron lung."

No one disputed this.

My junior year I broke my all-time relationship record by dating one boy for an astonishing two years. Though, to be truthful, I was never completely faithful. I am embarrassed to admit that even though we were together for so long, I could never call him "my boyfriend" without coughing. God knows I wasn't going to use the "L" word—lover. Even thinking it made me blush. *Loverrrr,* that was a word actresses in foreign films used (and they always had more than one), a word you'd see on the cover of *Cosmopolitan.* It felt wrong in my mouth, flipping off the end of my tongue like some sort of organ meat I couldn't bring myself to swallow. I don't know why I thought parsing the term *boyfriend* made a difference . . . but it did, at least to me.

Perhaps it made me feel less self-conscious about the fact that I could look at almost any boy and find his face lovely, and that I could imagine what it would take to seduce him. Sometimes, I would. Sometimes it wasn't because I was sexually attracted to him, or even fond of him. Sometimes it was about stealing a boy from a girl I hated, it was about seeing if I could get that boy who seemed to regard me as socially beneath him to beg me to fuck him. It wasn't about the sex, which was never anything so special. It was about the power.

It wasn't until the end of my senior year of college, when I found myself in the bed of a boy who seemed put on this earth just to give women pleasure, that I understood sex as an obsession, sex as a sport and a pastime. It was a revelation.

Before this I'd only been with boys who'd treated my body like some sort of finicky appliance, twisting my nipples, pressing on my clitoris as though this alone would send me into some wild and frothy spin cycle. During oral sex boys had fallen into two camps, those who'd acted as though they'd been kissing the Blarney Stone—and now that they'd done it they were going to get lucky! Or those enthusiastic munchers who'd had their indelicate ministrations cut short by my pulling them up by the hair, biting my lip so I wouldn't scream, *"A vagina is not a sandwich!"*

Not that I wasn't sympathetic to their plight. I couldn't imagine how hard it would be to bring someone to orgasm through cunnilingus. It seemed not unlike attempting to pilot an airplane with your tongue. This boy, though, this boy—well, he could make a bad girl want to behave, and a good girl give it up. I did both happily. Sadly, or perhaps it was for the best, it was the end of the school year and we were moving to different cities. After all, now that I knew *that* kind of sex was out there, the world was a very different place.

Having great sex was like discovering olives that didn't come in a can. Wow. How had I lived without olives? How could I think I didn't like these? I was going to start eating olives. Lots of olives, all different sizes and colors.

After graduation I moved to New York City. Where many came to the city with big career plans all laid out, I didn't know what I really wanted to do. Maybe I'd be an actress, or an artist, or a DJ, or maybe just a writer. Where some people have life-lists for bird spotting, I began a life-list for sexual partners. I wanted to have sex with a black man, a Japanese man, a woman (perhaps a volleyball player), and twins. I wanted a much older man, a horny Norwegian sailor (but who among us doesn't want that?), and a mysterious stranger on a train. I wanted to have sex with a blind man while wearing a black mask, imagining that like the blind masseurs of India, his touch would be extraordinary. I wanted, and I wanted, and I wanted. Unfortunately, my timing was off. It was the late eighties and I was a bit late to the party. A friend's brother died of AIDS, and in my few months of working at Tiffany's (my first New York job), three men disappeared from the main floor. What was I to do? I did what any resourceful lass would do: I called up an old college boyfriend, the one I'd dated for two years—putting aside the fact that he'd once tried to have me committed, in part because I'd kept my money in my shoe. I was sure he was clean, and I knew he'd have sex with me. I told him I was coming to his town that weekend, and did he want to get together?

He did. That Friday after work I headed to Penn Station. It was a mob scene. Milling beneath the Departures and Arrivals

I spotted an intense-looking guy with unevenly cropped blondish-brown hair that stood up on end. He was wearing a torn-up Harris tweed coat, safety-orange socks, high-tops, black pants, and a turtleneck sweater. Sticking out of his pocket was a biography of Jean Cocteau. Slung over his shoulder was a gas mask bag.

I barely had time to check him out before they called my train. Walking down the steps to the platform, I heard a voice say, "This is hell, isn't it?"

It was the boy in the Harris tweed coat.

"It is," I said, my heart beating fast. I was suddenly aware of the large, dorky, tortoiseshell barrette holding back my ponytail, the stripe of white hair hanging in my eyes, my untucked turtleneck and linty black pants. I looked really awful.

He sat across from me on the train—a move I thought rather bold. I don't talk to strangers, I thought, staring at my feet, my cheeks and ears burning red. Who did he think he was? On our way south the train broke down repeatedly. During our six-hour journey he told me he was a writer and he was living in a crappy apartment on Staten Island, that he'd bailed out of graduate school a few weeks earlier, and that he now worked in an art postcard factory. To illustrate this point he reached into his bag and pulled out a postcard, a Robert Doisneau image of a French couple kissing on a bridge. I blushed. It was so corny, and so forward, and so . . . *sigh.*

"Take it," he said, when I handed it back to him. "It's for you."

BOOM. It was like a bag of flour fell on my head, and in that moment I thought, I will either marry this man or kill him, because no one else is ever going to have him.

I was elated, and I was crushed. How could it be?! I was confused. Settle down, I told myself. You've been wrong about men before. But it was hopeless. Something was different now having met this boy, it was like the air was different; the sun took days on end to set, nothing looked the same anymore.

I called up my old boyfriend and told him that I couldn't see him that night, that I'd met somebody.

"Really?" he said, sounding surprised and a little hurt.

"Are you joking?" my girlfriend said when I told her what had happened. "Watch it—you're going to marry him," she said, and laughed.

"Don't be ridiculous," I said. "I've known him one day."

Granted, I'd never been so unstrung by a boy in all my life, but still, I was a child, I couldn't go around falling in love, not now. What if I needed to sleep my way to the top? What if in one weekend all the people on my life-list appeared and threw themselves at me? What if? What if I kissed him and the world stopped for a moment, knocked off balance, and what if I had to kill him?

Two months later we moved in together. A year later we were married, at the age of twenty-three, my life-list out the window. I never looked back.

I said, *I never looked back,* I didn't say I *never look.* I look. Of course, I look. Pity the poor woman who doesn't look. I am happily married, not happily dead. Sometimes I will see a man buying a newspaper, or in a café, or fixing my phone line, and I will wonder what his kiss is like. What would it take to seduce him?

I wonder, What if I had never gotten on that train?

two dollars a word

～ precious williams

I knew every nugget of gossip there was to know about him I'd pored over the magazine clips, watched his so-called friends gleefully dish the dirt on him on VH1's *Behind The Music*. I now knew the name of his first-ever girlfriend and the (many) grievances of his last girlfriend and how reluctant he was to tip waiters. They all said he was ruthless. Ruthless and driven. But I'd never met him.

As a freelance celebrity interviewer, I know intimate details about the lives of most of the men I meet before I actually meet them. I make my living hanging out in hotel suites, grilling the likes of Lenny Kravitz and Colin Farrell for information that shouldn't be the public's business but is. It's my job to be armed with all of the facts *and* the pertinent gossip about a star before I sit down and switch on my tape recorder.

When I started doing this job I was twenty-five, and I approached each interview with a male celebrity as though it was a high school date. I'd invite my friends over to my flat the evening before the big day to help me decide what to wear and then call the same friends immediately after the interview to report back on what he said, what he was wearing, whether I was attracted to him or not, and whether he flirted with me. I never let it get sexual, though, and five years and two hundred interviews later, I'd learned it wasn't necessary (or advisable) to show up at press junkets in miniskirts and high-heeled mules. When a star flirted outrageously with me, it no longer massaged my ego. It simply emboldened me to go ahead and ask the sorts of intrusive questions that editors love and celebrity publicists fear.

But rappers were always tough interviews, no matter how flirtatious things got. Almost all film stars and models and pop singers can string a sentence together, but rappers—the very people who make a living out of their love of wordplay—become oddly monosyllabic when interviewed, answering every one of my questions with: "nothin," "just chillin," "y'know-what-I'm-sayin," or "holla." This makes for one-dimensional interviews and frustrated editors. But I was willing to work around some boring conversation for *this* assignment because it included a free trip to New York *and* it paid two dollars a word.

He was holding court at the Four Seasons, holed up in an ostentatious suite for the day, promoting his latest album. I was the last journalist to interview him on the last day of a three-day press junket. When I walked into his suite and his publicist announced, "Precious Williams, UK press" and then backed out of the room, he didn't even look up. He was sprawled on the cream damask sofa, much skinnier than he looked on his album covers, wearing baggy FUBU jeans. His big Nike-shod feet were planted atop a glass coffee table, on either side of a stack of glossy magazines. The lids of his almond-shaped eyes were lowered to the point where it wasn't clear whether he was awake or asleep.

I sat down next to him, switched on my tape recorder, and waited. His eyes opened a fraction, and his gaze slid to the right, resting lazily on my face, then my breasts, which he stared at for several minutes before smirking, reaching his hand into his voluminous jeans pocket and pulling out a half-smoked spliff.

He didn't offer me any of the weed, and the more he smoked the less able he seemed to answer—or even comprehend—my questions. "Which track on the new album is most personal to you?" I asked as he snatched up the remote control and started to flick between cable channels, ignoring my question and yawning loudly. I tried again: "What's your day-to-day routine when you're not recording or touring?" He looked at me incredulously and slumped back down on the sofa. "Nothin'," he answered finally. "Just chillin'."

"Did you always know you'd become a rapper? Was there ever anything else you wanted to do?"

He sighed heavily. "Nah. It was always about the music, y'know what I'm sayin'? Everybody always knew I wasn't goin' to do nothin' regular..." His voice trailed off. He checked the cumbersome Rolex on his wrist and stubbed out the spliff.

"You're pretty as hell, girl," he announced suddenly, making me drop my pen. "How old are you? You married? Got kids?"

I shook my head. "I'm twenty-four," I said, the lie rolling easily off my tongue. He looked skeptical. Like he didn't believe I was twenty-four or didn't believe I was childless. Or both. "Damn, girl," he said, animated all of a sudden. "You twenty-four and you ain't got no kids yet? What are you waitin' for?"

According to a recent *Vibe* interview I'd skimmed through in my room earlier, he had two kids by two different women.

"When did you last fall in love?" I asked, fumbling around on the floor for my pen.

"When you walked in the door," he quipped, grabbing my open notepad off the table and trying to read my hastily scrawled questions and notes. "You from London, England? Where you staying at?"

"Downtown. At the Mercer."

"I'm gonna give you my cell number," he said decisively, taking my pen out of my hand and scrawling his digits across an entire page of my pad.

"Yeah, sure. I'll, umm, call you," I said, my voice rising an octave with each word. I handed him my business card before leaving, but I didn't look him directly in the eye.

Cassie, the publicist from the London office of his record label, was marching around with a clipboard and acting like an officious junior high school teacher on her first field trip. She'd reserved a table for seven at 7 P.M. at the Mercer Kitchen and instructed all of us UK journalists to meet there for dinner. Unfortunately, she'd also planned an early start for the following morning: a 7 A.M. trip on the Staten Island Ferry, followed by a group visit to the Empire State Building.

Over drinks upstairs at the Mercer, Cassie (who was on her fifth or sixth Cosmo) announced that she was starting to feel like Carrie Bradshaw. "Shame you don't look like her," scoffed Nigel from the *London Times*. The hotel door opened, and Meg Ryan scuttled through the white voile curtains and up the stairs, her long blonde hair extensions fanning out behind her. "Sooooo thin," sighed Tamara from the *Daily Mirror*. "This is the fucking life," agreed Sam from *The Sun*, knocking back another martini.

Sam, always eager to steal his rivals' quotes, turned to me. "He was in a foul mood when I went in this afternoon, gave me a lot of attitude," he whined. "Did you get anything about the breakup with—"

I shook my head. "No. I didn't get much of anything at all," I said, toying with the idea of adding, "apart from his phone number."

I got back to my room after midnight, so tired I could barely keep my eyes open long enough to brush my teeth. The phone rang. "What you doin'? Want to come hang out at my hotel?" It was oddly disconcerting to hear whispering intimately to me over a phone line in the early hours of the morning the voice I'd listened to repeatedly on the radio. "How you feel?" he wanted to know. "I'm fine," I said, although I was anything but fine. I was excruciatingly exhausted, jet-lagged, and, hearing his voice again, nervous as hell. "Oh, I know you *fine*," he drawled. "But how you feel?"

I felt sticky-hot and slightly drunk and sort of sluggish, like I was moving through thick treacle as I took the phone into the bathroom to peer at my lackluster reflection in the mirror. I felt *old*. I'd already smeared a layer of night cream over my face and under my eyes, and the mere thought of taking a shower and redoing my makeup and shaving my legs so that I could wear my new denim skirt made me want to curl up in bed again and unplug the phone.

"So what time you comin' through?" he asked. It didn't seem to occur to him that I was a journalist, not a groupie, and simply not the kind of girl who would drop everything to go and "hang out" in some rap star's hotel room. At least this one was smoother than the *last* rapper I had interviewed. That one had ignored all of my questions, boasted of his plans to stop by Buckingham Palace to have his picture taken with the "royalty people," patted me on the butt as I'd stood up to go, and then sniggeringly tried to cajole me into giving him a massage—in bed.

I could hear his breathing on the other end of the line, but neither of us spoke for what seemed like five minutes. I wondered how a man so dynamic on stage could be so apathetic on the phone. And why did a star who had hundreds of models and groupies at his beck and call want to invite a prying journalist around to his hotel room in the middle of the night? "I'm sorry, I'm not that sort of girl," I said primly. He laughed. And then I laughed.

I'm also not the sort of girl to ever turn down an opportunity to snoop into other people's lives. So in the end, my curiosity propelled me into the shower, into my clothes, and into a cab. Sex was out of the question, I told myself several times as the taxi ambled along still-busy Fifth Avenue. I didn't know where he'd *been*, my period was about to start, and more important, I didn't even *know* him. I'd flirt with him, and I'd make him laugh, and coax some extra quotes out of him for my article, and then I'd leave.

The cab driver kept turning around and asking me questions in his thick Pakistani accent, but I could barely understand anything he was saying, and he seemed to be addressing the questions to my lap and not to my face. Was my skirt too short? Who was I kidding going to a man's hotel room in a miniskirt in the middle of the night? I looked down at my freshly shaven legs, glistening with body lotion, and remembered the first time I'd ever met a rapper, fourteen years earlier.

My then–best friend Sarah and I had been approached on the dance floor of a London nightclub by a road manager, whisked into the VIP section to meet a New York hip-hop duo, and then invited to ride in their limo and hang out with them at their hotel in Knightsbridge. Sitting side by side on a king-size bed in one of their hotel suites, Sarah and I had squeezed each other's hands, beaming in disbelief. Twenty minutes later, hot tears and black rivulets of mascara had rolled down my cheeks as I'd sprinted down the corridor, chased by a shirtless rapper. I could still hear him yelling after me: "Get your little butt back in here, girl!"

Now I ordered the cab driver to pull over, halfway between the hotel I'd just left and the hotel I had been going to. I handed him a twenty-dollar bill, leaped out onto the sidewalk, and started walking purposefully back downtown. I couldn't "hang out" in anybody's hotel room but my own tonight; I was completely out of my depth, just as I had been back then, when I'd been sixteen and still a virgin and one of the rappers had started trying to unfasten my halter top. "I think I'm out of my depth," I'd whispered to my friend Sarah, imploring her to leave with me. Sarah and the two men had looked up at my tear-stricken face and laughed.

Sarah had been only fifteen, but when she'd come to school the following Monday she'd boasted that she'd been screwing both of the musicians all weekend and hanging out backstage at their concert. I'd told our friends I thought Sarah was a slut, but for years afterward I wondered if I'd missed out on a once-in-a-lifetime opportunity. And now the opportunity to do the wrong thing was presenting itself again, which is why it seemed almost justifiable to turn around and head uptown. To his hotel.

Sex with a total stranger *is* totally sluttish, I reasoned. But surely sex with a star who could have any woman he wanted had to be an opportunity, of some kind or another. Surely it was better than no sex at all, and it had been almost a year since I'd had any (unless you counted the occasional drunken bout with my pathetically clingy ex-boyfriend). I turned and started walking purposefully toward the rapper's hotel.

He was staying in a boutique hotel in Midtown, nestled on a quiet block just off Fifth Avenue and so discreet that I walked past it three times. The corridor leading to his room was lined with contemporary art, and the hotel itself was all studied imperfection: exposed pipes and unfinished, vaulted ceilings. His penthouse suite had its own private roof terrace, where he led me as soon as I walked in the door. The evening was still stiflingly warm, the clinging August heat wrapping itself around my bare arms and legs. But I still shivered as I gulped down the martini he'd placed in my hand. He set his half-empty tumbler of Coke on the table, staring deeply into my eyes as I said something about London and my plans to move to New York.

Then he began massaging my shoulders, and I slumped against his chest, closing my eyes and sighing happily. "I don't usually do this," I murmered halfheartedly as he tilted me against the balcony, nuzzled against my neck, and slid his hand up my thigh. He turned me around, kissing me deeply as he untied my halter top and peeled it down over my bare breasts. I tried to wriggle away and then started to giggle. He held on to me and started sucking greedily on my left nipple. I arched my back, still contemplating squirming out of his grasp, doing up my top, running out of the hotel, and never explaining myself.

As if reading my mind, he scooped me up in his arms, carried me into his room, and dumped me on the bed, where he yanked off my skirt. His forcefulness excited me; I reached up and snatched off his baseball cap, pulled off his T-shirt, unzipped his jeans, pulled them down, and then slid my arms around his neck and kissed him hungrily. "Tell me what you want," he drawled as he unwrapped a condom. I blushed and avoided looking at him by burying my face into his close-cropped hair and pressing my body against his. "Tell me what you want," he demanded again, his breath becoming raspy and heavy as he pushed me back onto the bed and parted my thighs with his knee. "I want you to fuck me," I moaned as he entered me gently. "Harder."

"You're a godsend," he murmured into my hair, after. He sat up, stretched his long arms, grabbed the remote control from the bedside cabinet, and switched on the wide-screen

TV. "I'm not gonna let you get even a minute's sleep tonight," he boasted. And then we watched basketball in silence until he fell into what appeared to be a deep sleep, with his lanky frame scrunched up into the fetal position, his back to me and the sheets drawn possessively around him.

"You must do this with a lot of girls," I murmured stupidly, staring up at the ceiling. No reply. "How much longer are you staying in town?" I asked.

He groaned, opening his eyes halfway and peering at me. "You intendin' on stayin' here? I need to get some sleep, I'm tired. There's no point you bein' here."

But I didn't leave. Some strange, possessive instinct warned me that if I left, he might suddenly spring to life, get dressed, and go find himself another girl. So I lay there, feeling cheap and jet-lagged and waiting for him to wake up and fulfill his promise of not letting me get any sleep. At 5:00 A.M. shards of sunlight pierced through the linen curtains and he still hadn't acknowledged my presence, even though I'd prodded him in the back and whispered, "Wake up" into his ear every half hour.

The predawn light made it all look tawdry. He was sleeping with his mouth open, and his teeth looked ever so slightly yellow. My nail polish was chipped, stubble was forcing its way through the skin on my legs, and I couldn't find my hastily discarded panties (in fact, I had a vague recollection of him throwing them off the balcony the night before). I tiptoed knicker-less through the hotel lobby in my denim micro mini, feeling, and basically looking, like a cheap hooker.

My editor had told me to keep expenses down, so I waited for the downtown bus, putting on my Prada sunglasses as soon as I sat down. An old man sitting opposite me stared un-abashedly up my skirt, and I pressed my thighs together, pre-tending to study the chipped fuchsia nail polish on my toes. When I looked up, the man was still leering, and with a grunt he thrust his hand into his pants pocket and pulled out ten crisp dollar bills, holding them up in front of me like playing cards.

Just then my cell phone vibrated, and I jumped in my seat. It was my editor. "How did it go?" he wanted to know. "How much time did you get with him yesterday?"

"Great. He was great," I said, stepping off the bus at Four-teenth Street. My call waiting beeped. "I'm missing you al-ready," said the voice at the other end. "What you know about flying down to Miami for the weekend, leaving tonight? I wanna see you again, boo."

Presumably this was some sort of strangely worded invita-tion. Whatever it was, I didn't know how to respond. Scream-ing "Fuck you, you asshole" was an option. But so was "I want to see you again, too." I remembered my editor and pressed the Flash button on my phone. "The pictures have come back and they're great, so we're going to run it over five pages," he was saying. "I need you to get as much color and gossip on him as you can. You need to find out what hotel he's staying at, how he's treating the staff there, who he's sleeping with. You might have to stay another night or two to dig around."

I hit Flash again. "What's going on in Miami?" I asked in a tone that I hoped was civil but icy. "Are you doing a concert?"

"Nah, nothin'," he drawled. "Just chillin'."

in the bowl of lights that is la paz

ᐒ pam houston

He was fluent in five languages. That was the first thing. The second was that his name was Gabrielle. By the time he got to the line that sealed the deal—*An architect understands that the most stable point is at the junction of many stresses*—there were more than enough reasons to sleep with him. His good works, for instance, on behalf of the developing country where we both found ourselves (he was building a hospital to serve the Bolivian poor). His half-lidded chocolate eyes and the dark hair that fell in a kind of Jackson Browne–ish way across his forehead and into them. There was Palermo, his home, and the fact that my mother, the actress, had had her most tumultuous romance with a man from Palermo.

My mother had died only a few months before my trip to Bolivia, just a few weeks before Richard Nixon had had his stroke, and I had started to entertain the notion that after a person dies they are allowed to amuse themselves by wreaking havoc with some still living person's life. My mother had hated Richard Nixon more than anyone, and I wondered briefly if she had sent the architect from Palermo to me—and if the gesture had been a blessing or a curse.

The architect wore a wedding ring, which at the time, I was much too young and heartless to take into consideration. He bought me a pair of flat silver hoops, carved with llama shapes, from the witches' market in La Paz. I have never thrown them away, even though they are long past tarnished and have almost returned to whatever underground form the cheap silver took before it was mined and fashioned. This tells me something, although I am not entirely sure what.

I was on assignment in Bolivia for a travel magazine. I was five days into a twelve-day trip, and the photographer who was traveling with me had already successfully picked up and bedded two other men—"oil guys," she called them, whatever that meant. It was the photographer who had noticed Gabrielle in the lobby, and the photographer who had asked him to join us later at a local bar.

Although I was traveling often and widely in those years, sex in third world countries was not something I actively sought out; this was due to some combination of fear of disease, shyness, and the simple fact that at five feet seven inches, and anywhere from 155 to 175 pounds, I was simply bigger than most of the men in most of the countries I visited. But Gabrielle stood well over six feet tall and was pleasantly broad and sweetly rounded (all his wife's gnocchi, no doubt), and he was a grown-up. Unlike the photographer I traveled with, I fancied myself a grown-up too.

We were talking about Bhutan, a place both Gabrielle and I had been, and loved, when the photographer interrupted to ask Gabrielle what he liked best about making love to a woman.

If he was surprised by the question he didn't show it; he only leaned back on his bar stool, pulled the plastic straw he'd been chewing out of his mouth, and said, "I don't think about making love to a woman. I think about making love with a woman."

"Oh, please," I said, "give me a break," and that turned his attention from the photographer back to me.

"No, really," he said. "When I am making love with a woman, it is her pleasure I am concerned with, far more than mine."

I was still skeptical, but both the photographer and I moved our chairs a little closer to him. The photographer was younger, thinner, and more flirtatious than me. We were both single, but her singleness seemed to have an urgency about it that I rarely felt, and the thought of competing with her over Gabrielle exhausted me before we had even begun. I fully expected that the trip would continue as it had been—the photographer out and about until all hours, me with my book on Quechua myths, holding down the fort—and I was pretty sure that would be fine.

Then Gabrielle started talking about the hospitals he had built in Mongolia, in Laos, in Zaire, and Malawe. For me, place names have always been the greatest aphrodisiac, and he had a whole alphabet of stories at his disposal: concerts in Athens, fireworks in Brindisi, a motorbike in Cairo, a camel festival in Dakar.

On top of everything, Gabrielle could dance, and when the salsa band started, the three of us danced ourselves silly, drinking huge goblets of the golden national beer called Pacena, shandy-like in its lightness. It was during the band's second break that he said the true and sexy thing about stability and stress.

Many hours later, during the all-important elevator ride, I was pretty sure that I had won the undeclared competition. Gabrielle had asked me for the last dance, he'd made a point of sitting next to me in the taxi, and now, as the little light jumped from floor to floor, he rested his hand warmly in the small of my back. Then he leaned over and spoke close to my ear about the possibility of a threesome.

I pretended not to understand him while I tried to decide what to do. Kicking him in the groin was one option, striding purposefully away when the elevator door opened was another. A threesome was neither in my repertoire nor on my list of hoped-for experiences. What staggers me now (six years of therapy later) is why it didn't occur to me to simply say no.

Gabrielle waited through six floors of silence before speaking more plainly, and louder. The photographer nodded enthusiastically (no wonder I never had sex when I traveled!), and I was ready to concede, happy to get off at our floor—the doors were opening even as I was formulating my little concession speech—and leave them to go up to Gabrielle's penthouse together. But he had seen that his question had hurt my feelings, and he put one hand on the open door button and the other on the nape of my neck and said to the photographer, "I was only kidding, of course. Good night, sleep well."

He took his hand off the button and the doors began to close, and the photographer slipped out and once again we were climbing.

As it turned out, Gabrielle was not, in fact, more interested in a woman's pleasure than his own, unless, perhaps, he thought it pleasurable for a woman to give a twenty-minute blow job while alternately freezing and drowning under a full-on shower, her knees rocking on the cheap, hard porcelain of a cheap, penthouse tub. (And he may have thought just that.)

The most tender thing Gabrielle did all evening was before the shower, when he pulled me back urgently from where I hung over his balcony looking at the bowl of lights that is La Paz (downtown is in the bottom of a canyon, and the suburbs climb the steep hills on all sides), saying, "Come away from there this minute! I know how poorly these buildings are made!"

When my mother and her lover from Palermo went back to the old country to meet his family, they fought almost constantly. "See there," she would say, showing me pictures of the two of them smiling brightly in front of the Leaning Tower of Pisa, in front of the Duomos in Rome and Florence and Milan, "Right there we were just about to kill each other," and "There, right before that one, I had made him promise to take me to the airport so that I could go home."

She did end up coming home without him, his mother's spaghetti recipe tucked into her passport. Anchovy paste, hot Italian sausage, and a bay leaf were the key ingredients, she always claimed; before too long it became my father's favorite dish. She never quite got the Italian out of her system, though, and one time, exactly at the age I least wanted to hear it (eleven, twelve?), she told me that it had all been worth it because of the sex.

If Gabrielle and I had sex, as in intercourse, as in comfortably, on his hotel room bed—and I can't think why we wouldn't have—the memory of it is lost to me now. I remember quite intensely, though, what a delightful conversationalist he was, no doubt in any one of five languages; and the color of the shower tiles . . . an almost neon green; and the texture of that lock of near-black wet hair that fell over his determinedly closed eyes as I kneeled below him; and the tiny white lights, like the sky turned upside down, that stretched out in every direction as I leaned over the flimsy railing of Gabrielle's penthouse balcony.

sexual healing

ᴇᴠᴀ daisy garnett

The tale I am about to tell took place mostly in Paris, but for me, it is a New York story. I am English and have lived in London for almost a year now, but for most of my twenties New York was my home. I went there for a week when I was twenty-three and stayed seven years. Sex had a lot to do with that. It was, in many ways, my calling card. I was in a strange country, entirely unwatched, and I wanted to have adventures. I didn't plan to settle down but hoped instead to have as good a time as possible, and to return home when I had to—when the fun, spare couches, odd writing jobs, and free dinners ran out. Of course, things don't work like that. Odd writing gigs turned into a job and a work visa, spare couches turned into sublets and leases. New York became my home, and I thought, If I am lucky enough to live in New York, I have to *live in New York*. I wanted to converse with writers and artists one moment, dance with drag queens the next. I wanted to be able to waltz into any restaurant, bar, or club and feel at home. I wanted to experience the New York of the women I had read about—Edie Sedgewick, Debbie Harry, Diane Brill, Nell Campbell, Tama Janowitz—women whose magazine photographs I had poured over growing up at home in rainy England.

This translated, more or less, into wanting to have sex with the whole city. I had sex with DJs and club kids, actors and wannabe rock stars, performance artists and painters. I fucked a junk dealer, a magician, a teacher, a scriptwriter, a playwright, a couple of bankers, and several writers. I slept with an art critic who woke me up early the next morning to take me to the Met before it opened, a rap star during a recording session of what became a hit song, a lawyer who took Viagra, and a lesbian on the cold, piss-stained stairwell of her coke dealer's Alphabet City apartment. Luckily, a lot of the city did not want to have sex with me.

Though I told myself I was having a blast, I often felt exhausted, empty. Like many women, when it came to sex I was so grateful to be given the opportunity to say yes that I never learned how to say no. Saying no, I thought, meant "he" went off into the night thinking, She's a prick tease; She's frigid; I don't like her; She's no fun. Such perceptions I *would not allow*. I knew in my head that it was time to take more care with my life and my sex life in particular, but I had trouble spreading the good word through the rest of my body. Ironically, it was through my most "casual" encounter that I began to wise up.

It happened when I had just left a job at a magazine and was eager for freelance work. An editor at a glossy magazine asked me if I would do a story on the cult of the "celebrity healer." Specifically, she wanted to know more about a healer she had heard about via some secret Deep Throat source. No one knew what kind of a healer this man was, or where his office was exactly, but he lived in Paris and treated two of the world's most famous rock stars. The editor had a cell phone number for him, but he'd never answered her calls. Still, the editor said, she was intrigued. If I could track him down, I could go to Paris.

As backup research, my editor sent me to another healer in Manhattan and put me on the phone with several lunatics in Los Angeles. The New York healer worked out of a room of unbelievable squalor. "Ah," he said as soon as he saw me. "Your aura is ringing like an alarm bell. It is shrieking at me. You could have so much, and yet you are unhappy and power-less. I see all these things around you, but they are out of your reach. You try, but you can't access them, can you?" I burst into tears. He was right. In many ways I had a lot. I was young, and living a shiny life in New York City. I was earning my living as a writer, I went out every night, had friends I adored, and knew people who threw parties. I was also alone, single, and jobless. For money I juggled stories, living from paycheck to paycheck. I was often bruised one way or another from en-counters with strangers and was always secretly awaiting the mysterious, nonexistent email or phone call that would change my life—or at least tether it down to a more secure spot.

I was curious and suspicious, then, about the Parisian

healer to the famous. I will call him Anton. It seemed a slippery profession, and, on top of that, he was elusive. Every day I called his cell phone and every day I left messages, but I never had any luck reaching him, until one Sunday afternoon he answered his phone. "Why, yes," he said. "Of course you can interview me. Come and have a treatment. I have to *show* you what I do. Only then can we talk. Come to Paris. Come this Tuesday." I got on the plane the next day.

Anton's office, which he shared with four or five other doctors, was the least New Agey place in the world. It was located in a smart part of Paris, and its waiting room was filled with bourgeois, middle-aged French men and women reading *L'Economiste* and wearing loden-mantels and loafers. I saw from a card that my healer was an acupuncturist and osteopath. This, I gathered, was serious stuff. Good, I thought. Perhaps I'll be properly healed. I sat down in the waiting room and watched with surreal detachment as a fabulously handsome man came bounding in. He looked like a French movie star—dark and compact, animated, and vital, glistening with good health and beauty. I, meanwhile, having just arrived on the red-eye, was tired and badly dressed. I looked plain and puffy and scrappily unprofessional. To my amazement this man-god came over to me and took me in his arms. He was my healer.

The first thing I did after he led me to his office and sat me down on—ah, I see—a massage table was to remind him who I was. "I'm the journalist," I told him, "the one who has come to interview you." I rummaged around for pencil and notepad to make my point. "Yes," he said, "I remember." He felt my pulse as he talked and squeezed my ankles and looked at my tongue.

"You are very tired," he said. " I am going to help you feel better. Once I have done that, we will talk. Now, I will leave you to take off your clothes. I will return and start work in a few moments."

Hmm, I thought. I *am* tired. I *am* ready for some magic. Did he mean take off *all* my clothes? I left my underwear on, lay down on the table, and covered myself with a handkerchief-sized towel as best I could. "Alors," he said, bouncing back into the room and whipping the towel away from me, "I begin. We take these off, too," he added, peeling off my knickers. So there I was, naked and tired, and pretty glad, actually, to be getting the massage of my life. It was the massage *of* life. It involved huge, generous glugs of olive oil and a lot of hot breath, both his and mine. As he darted around me, digging deep, I found myself at certain points in tears, at others laughing. Then, too, bits of me hurt a great deal, so much so that I would gasp for breath. It was such an intense and thorough massage, in fact, that it covered not only my outside but my inside too. That's right: My healer put his fingers up my ass. And my vagina. And not just a finger, come to that, a whole hand; what felt like an arm. At one moment I thought, Jesus, if I open my mouth his hand will appear through my intestines and out of my throat, like some horror movie pastiche. I had to work hard not to laugh. I was also in considerable pain. (It is interesting, no, that I stifled perfectly understandable reactions when he was working inside me but groaned loudly when he pressed my back and abdomen?) "Breathe, cherie," is all he would say. "Oui, oui. Good. Breathe. Ah, cherie, we are opening doors."

When I tell this story to friends, they interrupt me with

cries of protest. What was I thinking? they ask. Why didn't I stop him? they demand. The answer is, it didn't occur to me to stop him. I had given my body over to a doctor, and I didn't feel like reclaiming responsibility for it. Wasn't I embarrassed? one friend asked. Had I been to the bathroom recently? Was I clean down there? Well, I was embarrassed. I also felt shy. I am nervous about presenting my body at the best of times, and I have spent so many years resenting it (the usual womanly stuff: hips, thighs, belly too big; tits too saggy; legs too short, etc.) that I have often—always?—neglected to take much care of it. It is one reason I gave myself up so easily for so long (You want *this* body? *My* body? Take it. It's worth nothing to me), even though I knew empirically that most men aren't fussy when it comes to actual fucking. Everyone has a horror story to illustrate this. I remember one young man bragging to me about having drunken sex with a girl he found so unattractive that it was as much as he could do to fuck her from behind. "Man, I didn't even take my baseball cap off," he boasted, as if to prove he had real class.

But back to the healer with his hand inside me. Indeed, part of me could not believe what he was doing, and doing with such brisk, businesslike enthusiasm. Yet to say "Please stop what you are doing" would have also been to say "*Look* what you are doing." And anyway, if half of me was crippled by modesty, the other half thought, Fuck it, it'll do my body some good to have some healing hands not just on it, but inside it. God knows, I'd let enough strange penises rummage about inside there; it seemed about time a few internal feathers were smoothed down.

After three hours of this—exhausting—"massage," the

healer stuck a huge number of needles all over my chest, abdomen, and hips, switched on a hot light close to my body, and left the room. He told me that he would return shortly to put me back together. After twenty minutes I was still alone and restless. Every time I tried to move, the needles stopped being benign and I felt their pricks. After thirty minutes I became upset. I didn't like being trapped. Where was my healer? I wanted the needles off. I began to whimper and cry. Still no one came. After forty-five minutes I shouted for help. Finally a stranger in a white coat—a doctor, presumably—came in looking irritated. If he didn't have a cigarette dangling from his lips, he might as well have. He grunted at me and took out the needles, hurting me along the way. I felt upset and confused. I got dressed and went out to the reception room. "Where is Anton?" I asked the receptionist. "He has gone," she said blankly. "What about my interview?" I asked. "I don't know," she said, a study in French nonchalance. "Try him on his cell phone," she added. I gathered myself. I told her that I knew that to be a fruitless exercise since he wasn't in the habit of answering his phone. I said I would prefer it if she arranged a time it would suit him to take my call, and then to call me. I gave her the telephone number of my hotel, my mobile, and my apartment in New York. I told her that if I didn't hear from her, I would certainly be in touch. I explained that I had been flown to Paris at vast expense, and so far I had some very confusing data and no interview.

That evening I went out with friends, all of whom asked me why I was so wobbly, odd, undone, discombobulated. I blamed the plane journey and drank a lot of champagne. When I returned, fairly late, to my hotel room, the telephone

was ringing. It was the healer. Jesus, I thought, I have to interview the fucking guy now? I asked him to hold on while I
found my notepad. "No, no, cherie," he said. "We can't talk
now. Why did you leave? I wasn't finished. I must see you
again."

"Oh," I said. "Oh." I felt relieved. At least I would get my
interview now. I also felt excited. There was something about
the tone of his voice. I tried not to feel dread. I told him I was
leaving Paris at noon the next day. That didn't leave much
time, he said, so I should come in early. He would open the office especially. Could I come in at seven? I said I could. Could
we talk then? He said we could.

The next morning we greeted each other as old friends.
The office was empty. It felt sexy, being there. It *was* sexy. The
massage was different too. My healer didn't get gynecological
this time, but he was much more intimate. Hang on, I thought
as he worked on my nipples, isn't this sexual? No, no, I told
myself. How could it be? What presumption! He's a doctor.
He's wearing a white coat. I'm in France! It's the French way!
Not only that, he's devastatingly handsome. This is an important point. I'd always felt my looks weren't enough alone to en-
tice someone cold. And yet I prided myself on being adept at
the business of seduction. Getting laid for me was something
of a performance. Over the years I had constructed a persona—
nothing too excessive, nothing a million miles away from myself—and I'd gotten good at inhabiting it. I aimed to be dizzy
Daisy: blond and a bit undone with a candy-colored bra, a wel-
coming cleavage, and a good deal of skin on show. I aimed (and
I emphasize *aimed,* but certainly I often didn't pull it off) to be
festive and irresistible, like a sugarplum. To complete the

good-time-girl scenario, I never made demands, always had a good time, and worked hard to conceal any neurosis. I got in the habit of slipping away from my conquests at five in the morning and leaving a note to say thank you for the fabulous time I hadn't necessarily had. I hadn't employed any of my tricks on the healer. Far from it. I was there to work, not to seduce, and the idea that he would want to get frisky with naked, pale, unmade-up, untarted-up, push-up-bra–less me seemed absurd and impossible.

And yet wasn't he caressing my breasts? Surely it was sexual. It was. One moment I was second-guessing myself, and the next my healer was leaning down to kiss me, I was sitting up to kiss him, and he was as naked as I was. It didn't take long for us to have hot, dirty sex. At least, that is how I tell the story, because if you are fucking a celebrity masseur you have exchanged three words with, the sex should be hot and dirty. But honestly? Honestly I had a good time, but not *that* good. I didn't come, for example. But then, I didn't try to come. I lapsed into my good-time-girl persona—Look, Mum, see me on my Parisian adventure!—and I forgot, as usual, about satisfaction or fulfillment. I performed my part in this mini porn scenario and left it at that. And the healer? After our sex, as we began to dress, Anton began talking, spinning me lines. Stop, I wanted to say. We've done it, you don't need to do this. "Cherie, cherie," he said, "I feel you so strong. I kiss you so strong. Something happened, non? When will I see you again? When will you be back in Paris? When will we speak?"

"We will speak," I said, "we will speak tomorrow, by telephone. I have to interview you, remember."

"Of course," said Anton. "Of course. But what about next

month? I will be in London for four days. You must come, my love. I have such feelings."

"Maybe," I said, kissing him good-bye. "Now make nice to your other clients and don't sleep with *all* of them."

I was joking, I think. My masseur had fucked *me*. Presumably he fucked others. And yet something had happened. He seemed smitten. He was the one talking about feelings, not me. I was on air the entire train ride home. Other passengers stared at me as I randomly blushed or burst out laughing, thinking of how the buttons on my healer's white coat had pop, pop, popped off. Not only that, I had paid for my treatment. I had *paid*, I delighted in thinking, for sex. I sat on that train and I thought, Is this what it feels like to be a man? To hire a hooker, or to seduce, say, the woman in the lingerie store, to fuck her up against the mirror, tip her handsomely, and leave without wanting anything more? There was the matter of my interview, of course, but I was sure that would be dispensed with professionally and quickly. We would laugh about what had happened, I imagined. He would either tell me that fucking his clients was part of his treatment, in which case I had a story and a half (unlikely, since he did not advertise himself as a sex therapist or gigolo), or, more probably, he would tell me that what had happened between us was "special," I would momentarily believe him, and we would talk about how his rock star clients appreciated the healing powers of acupuncture and massage. As to whom he fucked and how often, I didn't care. I had gone in there a plain, unsuspecting client, and I had been swooped upon. Ironically, I felt empowered. It felt like a gift.

It felt less giftlike, however, when over the next few days

my healer did not return my phone calls. I left messages at his office and on his cell phone. The disaffected receptionist and I spoke daily, but Anton, she said, was either busy or out when I called. I left cheerful and reassuring messages. "It seems you don't want to do this story," I said, as a last measure, into his voice mail. "And that's fine. I understand. But if you could call me, then I can tell my editor for sure. I'm out most afternoons, so call in the morning if you want to talk or call later on if you would rather just leave a message."

The guy who doesn't call has happened to every girl; often to me, certainly. There is nothing to say about it except that it is horrible and disappointing. It took me a long time and a good amount of waiting by the phone to realize that you can be bedded by a man who is actually in the process of rejecting you. Why do they bother fucking you? Because they can. Because we let them. Still, each time it happens, and my healer was no exception, I wonder at the lack of manners. In this case it seemed especially rude. What was all that shit he had fed me about "feeling so strong"? What about some professionalism? (Rich, I know, coming from me.) He knew I was a journalist, knew I had visited him in order to write about him—didn't he worry that I was a loose cannon? Didn't he want to do some damage control? My Parisian adventure was beginning to leave a sour taste in my mouth. Not only that, I had some explaining to do. My editor, a smart, no-nonsense New Yorker, wanted to know why I couldn't write a simple article about a French healer, and the only way to explain was to tell her what had actually happened. This is a nightmare, I thought as I picked up the phone to confess my sins. Only it wasn't. She laughed and laughed, and made me pay for my exploits by having me research and write about every other celebrity guru on the planet.

But after coming clean to my editor, an interesting thing happened. I found myself less interested in sleeping around. After several years in New York, my lifestyle was no longer transient. Friends became more permanent. I moved to my own apartment with my own lease in Brooklyn. I started to see a shrink, and one of the things we talked about was my inability to say no to anything short term, and yes to anything that had potential to last more than a few hours. Eventually, I acquired a boyfriend—not for long—but it was he who left me after two months and not the other way round. He wanted to get married, he explained to an unamused me, and was looking for the One, which I was not. Perhaps it is no coincidence that I also began to think of moving back to England. I didn't want to leave New York, but my father was ill, my sister had had a baby, and a friend offered me a ride to Europe across the ocean on his sailboat. It seemed a good time to go home.

Before I left New York, however, I received a phone call. "My love," a French voice said. "*My love.* I am in New York and must see you." It was the healer, almost two years later. I was stunned. He told me he was in New York for the weekend only, to attend to one of his rock star clients. He said he was staying at the Trump International Towers Hotel, where I must meet him. I agreed. I had questions for him, after all, not the least being, Who are you? Rasputin? The next morning I brooded and planned my attack. This time, I thought, you will talk. But something happened the moment I saw him waiting for me in the lobby of his hotel. All my anxiety and anger fell away, all at once. "Cherie," said Anton, embracing me. I laughed. "We go to my room," he said, and I nodded. It was boiling outside. I hadn't been laid for a long time. I thought, You know what? I'm not interested in what this man does or doesn't do. I couldn't give a fuck. I am young, I want to be naked and I want to get off. I want to have proper hot, dirty sex with this strange, handsome French man. So I did. And it was good; properly good. This time I wasn't shy. I was demanding. I wasn't embarrassed. I didn't care about pleasing him. I did care about making sure he pleased me. I came. He didn't. Afterward he burst into tears. He reminded me of myself when I was a teenager in bed with my first love, back when every touch was deeply, tearfully felt. "Mon bébé," Anton said, squeezing me. I laughed. "Mon bébé et moi," he said with intensity. "My love," he said over and over again, "I love you. Cherie," he said again, looking at me hard, "I love you." I laughed, kissed him, and showered. I don't think I said more than two or three words.

Sleeping with my healer that New York afternoon was the perfect conclusion to my New York sex life. It was everything I had imagined zipless sex in the city to be: free, easy, delicious, filling, glamorous, even. We were in a hotel on Central Park, after all. And in the way only New York can pull out the stops and amaze you, so it did for us. Flashes went off in all directions as we walked down the hotel stairs, hand in hand like carefree lovers. The paparazzi had come to capture our glow. It was dazzling, and seemed entirely in order. Yes, yes, I wanted to say, giving the photographers a royal wave, it was a good orgasm, wasn't it, thank you so much. In fact, immediately behind us was the boy band *NSYNC.

And yet, for all that afternoon's perfection, I am glad that my New York sex life wasn't so slick or easy. I'm glad that I got into scrapes and, as a consequence, felt scraped. I may have pushed my breasts into too many tight bras and smiled my way through too many humping men, but the more I think about it, the more I realize that it wasn't all performance. That girl trying so hard to be festive? That girl was me. I also realize now how tiresome and puppyish I must have been: too complicit, too easy, too zealous, too needy, too self-denying. I'm trying not to be that girl anymore, and sleeping with the healer turned out to be an instrumental lesson.

When I recount the experience, people ask me what I think the healer is really about. I don't know, I say, it's a mystery. And it is a mystery to me still, right down to the fact that I even tell the story. After all, I spent years having casual sex, plenty of it outlandish, and I would sooner be eaten by crocodiles than dine out on the finer details of who put what fingers where, how and when. And yet I tell my healer story to strangers at dinner parties, as if it happened to someone else and I am just the bemused narrator who watched events unfold.

Occasionally people ask me if I was hurt by the first encounter in Paris: Did I mind that I was taken advantage of? Oh, I say, I was cross and upset about him not calling, but that happens a lot, and I am used to it well enough, but as for the rest, I had a good time. I could have stopped him at any time, I say. I am breezy as I relay my story, breezy and entirely unscathed.

Of course nothing is so simple. The fact is, I *couldn't* have stopped the healer. True enough, I didn't particularly want to. I was seduced—both by him and by the glamour of having an all-expenses-paid tryst with the subject of an article, in Paris, no less. But beyond that lurks a more sinister truth: It didn't matter what I wanted because I never—ever—factored that in. Much more important was, Will "he" be happy? Sleeping with the healer on that hot day in New York woke me up. It was revelatory because he showed me what it must have been like to sleep with my former self. He was keen, compliant, over the top, and eager to please: in other words, me. Whereas I, like any normal man, was grateful for his enthusiasm, didn't give a shit about his feelings, and was pleased to see the back of him.

Was it Marilyn Monroe who said, "No sex is wrong if there's sex in it"? It's a good line, and one that I buy into wholeheartedly. My healer experience didn't compel me to give up casual sex in one fell swoop. I'm single still, and if the mood takes me, I will go to bed with the occasional stranger. But I won't do it to please him or to prove my worth. Sex, for me, has stopped being a way to win approval. It is not, I have learned, a mark of an adventurous life. If I have sex, I want it to be thrilling, but I no longer rely on it for thrills. Instead I am learning the pleasures of staying still, the great intimacies in sustained friendships, and the rewards of hard work: of writing every day, and the adventure that language offers—not only through writing, but through speaking up. Saying no, these days, is as thrilling as saying yes.

a model boyfriend

∽ melissa de la cruz

I met him at one of those snooty, velvet rope clubs in Soho, in 1993. I was twenty-three, and I still remember what I was wearing: a leopard-print three-quarter-sleeve jacket (purchased from a thrift store in the West Village for forty dollars, with a label from the "Lady Taylor" collection), my Chanel earrings, real ones, with interlocking gold Cs glued onto the surface of each oversize pearl (a birthday gift from friends who pooled their money together so I wouldn't have to keep wearing my fake Chinatown ones), a black sweater, torn Levi's jeans, and my black patent leather John Fluevog Mary Janes, bought on sale. I was sitting in the back room, on a velvet ottoman, across from my best friend, Morgan, who was surreptitiously rolling a joint with his long, thin fingers.

It was a Saturday night, and we'd arrived at the club un-fashionably early, around nine-thirty, so that we would have no problem at the door. It was a useful trick for wannabes like us, whose names were never on the stringent guest lists that ensured admission after midnight, the peak period. The only downside was that for two or three hours, we were the only two people in the premises aside from the waitstaff. Around eleven or so, the floodgates opened. Suddenly, there were beautiful people everywhere—ordering drinks, dancing on the little coffee tables, chatting away in various Romance languages. The women were skinny and insectile, with fragile limbs and hard faces; their nipples poked through thin tank tops when they shook off their fur-trimmed brocade coats. The men wore black suits and jewel-colored shirts, massive gold Rolexes strapped to their hairy wrists, or else they were scruffy and unshaven, slouching in flannel shirts and Airwalk sneakers. Surrounded, Morgan and I sat on the couch with rapt expressions. This was the reason we went out. The reason we braved the dreaded "VIP-only" scene. We lived for the nights when we got lucky and found ourselves in the right place at the right time, when our evenings took on a cinematic turn. Maybe Madonna might pop in, or else Isaac Mizrahi and Sandra Bernhard, who were just as good.

I tapped out a cigarette from my pack and felt gratified.

"Do you have a light?" a voice asked.

Experience could have told me that such a clichéd pickup line wouldn't bode well for a romantic future, but I didn't have a lot of experience back then. I was flattered, especially when I looked up and saw who had addressed me. The blond man leaning against the white column was easily six-two, with a languid, leisurely grace. He was wearing a white starched shirt, unbuttoned to the base of his tanned neck, and a black suit. He had the kind of face that was usually found smoldering on a *GQ* spread—sharp-angled cheekbones, a thin, straight nose, deep-set blue eyes, and thick, honey-colored lashes. He was easily the most handsome man to whom I had ever handed my lighter.

"Thanks," he nodded. He smiled at me—even, Chiclet-white teeth, glowing in the dark. "Fantastic jacket," he said, nodding at my leopard-print coat. I think I said something then, something silly and predictable, like, "Social smoker?" or perhaps something that rivaled the banality of his opening gambit, like, "Come here often?" My confidence surprised me, since I was usually too intimidated by good-looking men to attempt conversation, and not one guy in any of the exclusive nightclubs I frequented had ever approached me before.

In any case, he took the liberty of sitting next to me on the velvet ottoman after that. Morgan raised his eyebrows, and for a while I was scared that the gorgeous man would turn out to be more interested in my friend than in me. Except that he didn't look gay at all. What he looked was Continental, from the Old World. He was meticulously well groomed, like Cary Grant, but he had a rakish air, like the Marlboro Man, a cowboy on leave. Morgan handed him the roach, and he took a puff, then passed it politely over to me.

He asked me if I had seen any of "the shows." It took me a minute to figure out that he was talking about Fashion Week. Apparently we had stumbled upon an after-party for a designer. I pretended I'd seen the Betsy Johnson spectacle I'd read about in *The New York Times.* He had a slight accent—

Swedish? German? Swiss?—that I couldn't quite place. He told me his name was Fritz, and that he had "walked" two shows for the men's collections. The black suit he was wearing was a tuxedo. I noticed the tie stuffed in the jacket pocket. I told him I was a writer, but I didn't mention that I had never been published.

I gave him my number on a matchbook. He called me the next week. I played the message several times, giggling at the way he pronounced my name, ("Meh-leeee-zuh"), like some cheesy European swain in a 1940s black-and-white film caper.

I was thrilled but anxious as hell, since I instinctively understood that dating a guy like him would involve a lot of pretending. Pretending I was a successful fashion journalist (I was a computer programmer). Pretending that I had the kind of life that involved friends who owned Soho lofts and threw casual parties attended by culturally significant and professionally attractive people. I didn't. But it was the life that I aspired to, with my Shabby Chic catalogs and fantasies of becoming Michael Musto's best friend—a life that, in New York, seemed to be tantalizingly within reach. For our first date, I begged my friend Lauren, who was an assistant to a famous graphic designer, to throw a party at her office, a loft in the West Village (close enough to Soho!). Since I guiltily didn't want to introduce Fritz to my real friends—grungy recent college grads toiling in entry-level positions—for fear they'd mar the decadent assumptions he was beginning to make about me from my clothes and the glamorous lies I fed him, I strong-armed Lauren into inviting her boss's friends instead—a more appropriate group comprised of interior decorators, artists, and editors at *Elle Décor* who would fill the smart and chic bill.

Fritz was suitably impressed. We breezed into the party and breezed out. Lauren was slightly miffed. (We didn't stay to sample her Earl Grey soufflé.) We had another party to go to, because with Fritz, there was always something else on the agenda. A magazine launch or a cocktail party at a new boutique. That night, we wound up tossing back gin and tonics at a rooftop "thing" in Tribeca, and then I invited him home. As the cab whizzed by the parking lots and personal storage warehouses in the far West Village, I closed my eyes and buried my head in his neck, grinding my hips against his jeans, my knees straddling his thighs, my skirt inching up to my waist. His hand reached underneath my blouse, then between my legs, as we necked all the way to my apartment. I caught my breath and pulled away, dizzy. At a red light, he leaned back and laughed.

"You're one of those wild girls, aren't you?" he said.

Sure. Wild. Why not? I thought as I awkwardly clambered off him, yanking down my skirt and reaching for my handbag to pay the smirking driver. Fritz eased out of the backseat— one smooth motion—and offered me his hand as I struggled out, all jelly legs on my five-inch platforms.

He was the first guy I'd ever taken back to my cramped one-bedroom, where I'd spent two years of lonely Sunday nights reading *War and Peace* and then masturbating to hazy movie-star fantasies. We climbed up the rickety stairs that always smelled of Chinese food, and stumbled inside, onto the futon-as-couch in my living room. I took my clothes off myself, in a frenzied, unembarrassed rush, unbuttoning my silk blouse and tossing aside my worn beige bra. I didn't want to waste any time waiting for him to do so. I didn't want him to change his mind. I also didn't want him to get the wrong idea. Like that we were just friends or something. (As if I had anything to worry about, after my performance in the taxi.) Still, I came on stronger and stronger, playing the part of some modern geisha girl possessed of kinky Far Eastern bedroom secrets.

I could sense his exhilaration, his growing excitement. He lifted me up in his arms, thrusting, searching vainly for an empty wall to press me against. Finding none, he dropped me on my tiny black IKEA dining table. I must have looked drugged, dazed, ready for anything in any position. He turned me around, bent me over, fucked me from behind, which I'd never done before. He groaned, he grimaced, sweat beads dropped onto the table. But he still wasn't through. When we finally made our way to the frilly daybed in the back room, exhaustion began to set in, and things became distant, mechanical. He flipped me on my back, held my legs high and tight, and made incremental adjustments as to friction, elevation, rhythm. I remember thinking it seemed he'd performed exactly the same sequence of manipulations many times before.

I never closed my eyes, preferring to watch him watching me. At times, it felt like it was happening to someone else. He held my legs so forcefully that yellow bruises would later bloom on my thighs and I'd be sore for days. We kept going, on and off, for three hours. But he was too drunk to come.

"You live in the bathroom?" he asked afterward, as I rested my chin on his chest. My Carmine Street one-bedroom had a unique layout—a tiny toilet sat in the corner of the living room (so small that you had to sit sideways on the seat to fit), and the shower stall was in the bedroom. Fritz's English wasn't very good, so I didn't bother to explain that it was the other way around, that I lived in a bedroom that happened to have a shower in it, not a bathroom that happened to have a bed in it. Then he slept and I spent half the night awake, memorizing his face.

It wasn't all about his looks. Okay, I'm lying. In all honesty, I derived great satisfaction from looking at him and basking in the reflected glory of his dazzling physical appearance. This is an understatement. After our first date I rang all my friends, announcing that I WAS DATING A MODEL! Of course, I found out later that he was also a waiter—at Maxim's on the Upper East Side, part-time, but still. He had a portfolio. He had done ad campaigns. He was German, twenty-seven years old (which seemed ancient to me back then), and he lived in a town house off Washington Square Park, with an older couple who rented him a room. He had three dogs: a Rottweiler, a German shepherd, and a Maltese. He wasn't vacuous or particularly vain. (Unlike the goofy space cadets in the movie *Zoolander*, he didn't drink orange mocha frappuccinos.) He painted canvas monochromes during his spare time, which struck me as being clichéd, though I'm not sure why. He was very sweet. He was always broke. Or maybe he'd just become too accustomed to people picking up the tab, cutting him breaks. (The elderly couple charged him two hundred dollars a month for rent.)

With Fritz, I was able for the first time to imagine myself as sufficiently attractive to the opposite sex. It was a revelation. I'd had a few boyfriends, but my most meaningful relationships were with homosexual men. Fritz changed things. I noticed men were becoming increasingly receptive to me.

Platonic male friends that I'd had secret crushes on but who'd been content to keep me at arm's length reacted to my newly elevated status as the girlfriend of an alpha male by acting jealous and possessive. I now understood what the word *covet* meant. Fritz was coveted, not only by me but also by most women, and I'd gained an enviable status by being his girlfriend. This was both obnoxious and intoxicating. My rivals would stare as much at me as at him—and I would be surprised at what I saw in their eyes: jealousy, surely; hostility, of course; but also admiration. At nightclubs, women would sidle up to me in the ladies' room and compliment me on my hair, my shoes, ask to borrow my lipstick. They seemed intent on figuring out what it was about me that had captured the attention of such a worthy specimen.

With Fritz, I could walk into any bar or nightclub and I would always get in, even if we arrived after midnight. He knew everybody—the bouncer at Café Tabac, the guy who ran the parties at Robots, the girl who held the clipboard at Spy. I measured my life in free drink tickets. It was just another way to escape from the dull, soul-crushing monotony of my career in systems programming. Fritz was my passport to the glittery and privileged world I desperately wanted to join but didn't know how to on my own.

One night, I arrived at a bar to meet him and found a lanky blonde clinging to his arm, laughing. The two of them were almost the same height, dazzling, otherworldly creatures. I felt short and used. But then he turned to me and gave me a small, secret smile. I felt elated. As if a spotlight had shone and I was transformed into their equal.

Back at my place, I led him into the shower stall, where I

knelt down, let the water run over his erection, and swallowed him whole. I wanted to show my appreciation, even if my knees turned red from scraping against the plastic. He grabbed the shower door for balance, his face clenched in orgasm, his knees buckling beneath him. Afterward, he absentmindedly patted me on the head. "That was really great," he said, toweling off as I brushed my teeth in the sink. He kissed me on the cheek and made himself comfortable on the futon, turning on the TV to a *Star Trek* rerun.

After that night, I started wishing he had something more to say, about politics, literature, or books—or that those topics would even come up in conversation. It began to occur to me that Fritz never paid for anything, and that half the time, I couldn't even understand what he was saying. We communicated through hand gestures and overly enthusiastic nodding. We said hello by tumbling into bed—sex was the first thing we would do before we did anything or went anywhere. His good looks became a backdrop, something I took for granted. I started referring to him as a "waiter" rather than a "model." He wasn't dumb, but he was certainly detached. Nothing bothered him. I began to realize that Fritz never made me feel beautiful. He was beautiful, which, since we were together, I took to mean that I was too. But I realized I wanted a guy who would make me feel beautiful when I was *apart* from him too. Part of me was cruelly looking forward to the inevitable day when he would become a great anecdote I could tell at dinner parties.

A few months after we broke up, I was sitting in a red leather banquette in the current "hot" restaurant with a new group of friends, a sprinkling of boldface names among them, at yet another over-hyped Fashion Week event. I had finally retained a gig as a fashion writer for a local paper. But as I tittered at the bitchy bon mots being tossed around (meanspirited references to certain models in rehab, how much weight André Leon Talley had gained, and so on), I started to feel a little ill from the overly sweet cocktails, and my eyes watered and burned from the dense fog of cigarette smoke. Now that I had finally reached a place where I would be more than welcomed at the very same clubs and parties to which I had desperately wanted entrance, I longed to be at home, or hanging out with friends who couldn't care less who the Sykes sisters were. I had imagined that happiness constituted a life ripped off the pages of glossy magazines, and that the perfect boyfriend was one that all the other girls would die to call their own. How little that added up to, now.

I excused myself to the ladies' room, where some of the group had hid in order to pass around a small brown vial of cocaine, dipping into it with long pinky fingernails. "Hit?" I shook my head. "Suit yourself," they shrugged. One of them asked if I was the same Melissa who had dated Fritz, the model. I nodded as I rooted in my bag for lip balm. My lighter—the silver Zippo with a Harley Davidson emblem that Fritz had admired the first night we met, fell out to the sink. "That is so cool," one of the girls gushed. I shrugged. I had bought the lighter in order to attract a certain kind of guy. "You like it?" I asked. "Keep it." They invited me to the next fabulous destination—an after-after-party at a photographer's studio in Chelsea, but I declined. In the cab, on the way home, I sunk back on the cracked vinyl seats in relief, willing the traffic lights green all the way downtown.

suddenly single

め liz welch

I thought I was going to marry William.

We met freshman year in college, in Shakespeare 101. He had shaggy blond hair and pale blue eyes and said smart things in class even though he never read the assigned books— a trick he'd perfected at Exeter. I took fastidious notes and read each text twice, certain that if I didn't, the powers that be would realize their terrible mistake in admitting me to Dartmouth, my first pick and furthest reach, and William's safety. He ambled around campus with a cocky bounce, wearing his signature army-green suede jacket, acquired at a flea market in Paris. He listened to the Grateful Dead and was the ringleader of a crowd made up of trust fund kids and European royalty. I couldn't believe he liked me, the girl who wore tapered acid-wash jeans with oversized sweaters to cover thick thighs. The public school girl who had never heard of Exeter before him, who worked in the campus grocery store and actually enjoyed studying at the library.

And yet, every day in class, I felt his gaze. When I was brave enough to meet his eyes, he would break into a sweet smile. I wound up sitting on his lap in his friend's overcrowded car on our first date to an off-campus party. There in the dark, squished in between sophisticated girls who'd grown up in New York City and the boarding school boys who wanted to bed them, William laced his arms around me.

Less than a year into our collegiate romance, during an extended family dinner at his parents' country estate, William's mother, well into her wine, announced that she hoped "Willy would marry Liz."

The comment stunned me at first, but as I scanned the golf- and tennis-tanned faces that ringed the table, the jolt softened to a numbness that made me feel oddly safe. This is a life I could slip comfortably into, I thought. It may even be exactly what I want. Ha! Only nineteen, and I had met my mate. Cross that off life's laundry list.

And yet he was only my first real boyfriend. The first man to challenge me intellectually and introduce me to the opera. The first man I spent whole nights with, said, "I love you" to and went on the Pill for. The first to cheat on me while I spent my junior year abroad in Edinburgh, and the first to tell me he was no longer attracted to me after I gained fifteen pounds from too many midafternoon hobnobs and evening pints of lager. He was also the first to wipe away my carefully applied lipstick as we were on our way to meet new friends for dinner—demanding, with a sneer, just who was I trying to impress?

We moved together to Hong Kong, where I, then a twenty-four-year-old high school English teacher, often found myself wondering what had happened to the sinewy young man who had once worn a red star of China cap and recited Che Guevara's life story to anyone who'd listen. The same man who'd run an inner-city literacy program back in Washington, D.C., was now a publishing executive who spent golf weekends in Phuket and evenings sipping Chivas Regal at private men-only social clubs. Soon the occasional line of cocaine became a weekend habit, and then I overheard one of his new friends talk about the Chinese with a scowl. That's when I panicked and began to plan my exit.

I moved to Manhattan to start a career as a writer, and William stayed in Asia. He was in Beijing on business the day I left, and so we said good-bye over a crappy phone connection. And while we decided not to break up but instead "take a breather," we both knew the end was in sight. As I boarded the plane, I felt like a racehorse being led to her starting box.

Within six months of my arrival in New York, I'd shed ten pounds without trying and landed a rent-controlled apartment on Washington Square Park. I found a nonpaying gig as a fiction reader at the *Paris Review*, then an editorial assistant job at a publishing house. With my first paycheck, I swapped my faded, flowing peasant skirts for micro minis in assorted animal prints, which I wore with platform sandals and tight T-shirts. I discovered pedicures and kept my lips glossed Cotton Candy Pink before 6:00 P.M., Tawny Taupe or Plum Wine thereafter. For the first time in seven years, there was no one to wipe it off.

Not only did I not miss William but I also realized how

much I had been missing *because* of him. After three months in book publishing, I was (miraculously) handed a plum job as an editorial assistant at *Vanity Fair*. It was there that William and I officially and rather pathetically broke up via email. I sent a message suggesting we take time off, and he replied in a business memo format.

TO: Liz
FROM: William
RE: breakup.
I think this is for the best.
All best, William.

I was at work, hidden by a particle-board partition, while the office hummed and buzzed just beyond. Phones rang, Xerox machines jammed, the mail trolley rolled down the narrow carpeted halls, past frazzled editors. I sat still and purposively tensed my stomach, gritted my teeth, and squinted my eyes in an attempt to drum up an emotional response to this limp and fizzled finale. Nothing. Not one tear. But then, as if somehow summoned by the physical strains, a panic rose from my belly and coughed up rapid-fire chunks of worry: Oh my God, what have I done? Did I just fuck things up royally? Did I blow my chance at a jet-set lifestyle—summering on the Connecticut shore, sipping chardonnay with sunny blondes in Lilly Pulitzer prints? Oh, and what of the long weekends in the little apartment in Paris, the heart-to-hearts with his down-to-earth-despite-it-all mom? The adorable towheaded kids we would inevitably have? The freedom to "work on my book" with no worries of making the rent?

But following that nauseating wave was an intoxicating

epiphany: I was no longer William's girl. I was free. Free to flirt, free to bed tall, dark handsome men, free to sleep with strangers and fuck cute boys in bathroom bar stalls and French kiss girls in downtown clubs. I was free to make up for the fact that for the past seven years, I had slept with only one man. That evening, I bounced home from work with both eyes open for anyone who would help me make up for lost time.

And so it began.

I started with Michael, a poet I had met while working at *The Paris Review,* who wore a black turtleneck despite the stifling summer heat. He had a tight halo of neat brown curls, big basset hound eyes, and a broad chest from the construction job he worked on the weekends to pay for his love of poetry. He was quiet and fidgeted with his hands when he spoke, his eyes always searching for a spot on the floor to steady his nerves. We went to see Johnny Depp as Ed Wood, and then afterward for fish-and-chips in an East Village pub, where Michael continued to fidget with his hands as he emoted in spastic bouts about Billy Collins and Octavio Paz. Though he was sweet, I felt not one of the hoped-for clichés—no butterflies in my stomach or lump in my throat or impulse to avert my eyes from his for fear of blushing. What should have been a dreamy date fell flatter than the warm tapped brew I sipped slowly to get through the night, which seemed to never end.

Then came Sam, the former, fleeting boyfriend of Susanne, my best friend from college. He was handsome, with chiseled cheekbones and a tangle of Jim-Morrison-in-his-leather-pants brown hair. We ran into each other at a party, and I, caught off guard by his piercing green eyes and well-toned torso trapped beneath a tight T-shirt, agreed to meet for sangria and tapas the following night. Things were off to a good start until out came the monologue: His mother died when he was sixteen, he was still recuperating and searching for that soul mate to fill the void. . . . And I suddenly remembered why he and Susanne didn't last. Too much work! Too needy! I just wanted to have fun, perhaps a romp in the sack, run my fingers through that hair, feel the thrust of those tight hips against mine! But no, he was looking for someone to salve old wounds. The more he pontificated on the destiny of our meeting—I too had lost my mother at a young age, could it be fate?—the more sangria I sucked down. By the evening's end, blurry-eyed and now deaf to his righteous rap, I still invited him home in the hopes he would shut up once we started to strip. Foiled again! Sam informed me that sex would ruin the connection he felt we had, a connection that needed to be savored until we met again. I scratched him off the list.

Benji was a bit better. We met at a wedding, where neither of us could keep our eyes off this unbearably sexy and thin French woman in a bubble gum pink bouclé miniskirt and matching jacket. She was slow dancing with herself, as if daring a potential lover to cut in. And so, perhaps because Benji was still interested in me while in the same room with her, I found myself leaning into him as we talked, even though he was so tall and so skinny that his large, crooked nose resembled a flamingo's beak. But he was also forward and flirtatious. He asked me for my phone number, and we met for dinner the following week, and then again to rollerblade through the city at midnight, and then again for drinks in Soho.

It had been three months since William and I had broken up, and I still had not kissed a man, let alone had the night of sweaty sex that had become my objective. While Benji was not the man I had scripted—his thighs were half the size of mine, for starters—he became more attractive with each sip of the caipirinhas he kept ordering for me. After my fourth, he had metamorphosed into the man of my drunken dreams. He was downright adorable! Those ears! That nose! I began licking his face at the bar. Literally. He practically had to carry me back to his apartment, stopping every so often so we could make out against anything steady—store grates, street-crossing posts, mailboxes. In his apartment, he pushed me onto his futon and then, to my dismay, derailed the sheer silly ecstasy of the moment by pulling out his penis; it was long and skinny like him, which I found hilarious. And then sad. And then gross. In seven years, it was the only one other than William's I had seen, let alone touched. That fact, coupled with the look on Benji's face—which I believe was the deranged disbelief of a man about to get laid by a woman he hardly knew—and I simply could not go through with it. So in a drunken haze, and perhaps out of guilt, I gave him a fast and foul-tasting blow job. And then I passed out. The next morning Benji, whose nose seemed to have grown larger overnight, was propped up on one elbow with freshly brushed teeth, urging me to take the day off work to "play." Head pounding and mouth carpeted with sour-lime-juice-laced-with-spunk-sludge, I managed to bolt from bed and into my rumpled clothes. I mumbled something about a work meeting, thanked him for the evening, and said yes, of course I would call.

Suddenly, being single was not as thrilling as I had hoped. Strike three had left me, both literally and figuratively, with a bad taste in my mouth. More and more, I found myself thinking of William, wondering what he was up to and if I had made a terrible mistake.

Then David called, and I perked up. We'd met freshman year at Dartmouth and had become close friends in Mississippi five years later during a yearlong postcollege teaching program. We had always flirted, but nothing more, because back then I'd been William's girl.

David was in town visiting his twin sister, an indie film phenom who had achieved a cultlike following among downtown hipsters. While the twins had been born and bred in Mississippi, he was a little bit country, and she was all rock 'n' roll, which was the prescription for a perfect Manhattan evening. He invited me to meet him at the after-party of the New York premiere of a much-talked-about independent film, and I thought, Free drinks, possible star sightings, and a handsome Southern boy who says "hot damn" when he's happy and "yes ma'am" when he's being polite? I could barely contain my glee.

The party, at a Midtown Irish pub, was in full swing when I arrived a bit late on purpose so as not to seem so overtly eager. I squeezed past a few vaguely familiar celebrities—was that Peter Gallagher?—and wove my way to the back of the bar where David's sister was holding court and he was slumped in a corner, nursing a Rolling Rock and looking bored as hell. His face lit up when he saw me.

"Let's get out of here," he practically yodeled as he grabbed my elbow and whisked me out of the bar and into a taxi. He then asked me for my address, claiming he was going to have to crash with me because his sister was in a fight with her boyfriend. The smirk he was trying to suppress made me know he was lying, but I loved the game and suggested we go first for a drink at a nearby bar. There, we sat catching up. He was finishing law school at Ole Miss and was more good ol' boy than ever. I was now the assistant to the editor-in-chief at *Vanity Fair* and was wearing three-hundred-dollar shoes. It was the perfect one-night stand.

When we got back to my apartment, the game continued. We talked for an hour, the tension wrapping itself around every word and gesture. Finally, he offered me a back rub, and I flung myself, belly first, on my bed. With a knee on either side of my hips, he began kneading my shoulders, bending down to whisper teasingly in my ear about all the Southern girls he had seduced in the same way. His warm, beer-tinged breath blanketed the nape of my neck, and I thought to myself, This boy has seduction down to a science, as I turned over slowly.

There was no deranged look on his face, just soft lips and hard chest and the delicious evening I had been hoping for.

The next morning, I was awakened with coffee in bed, and this time, genuinely sweet somethings whispered in my ear. I arrived late to work with a silly smile plastered on my face. David called a few hours later, wondering what I was doing for lunch, and while I wanted to meet up with him, I knew better. It had been a fling, the perfect one-night stand. He lived in Mississippi, I was staying in New York, and that reality made anything beyond our short-lived yet steamy tryst impossible. When he arrived at my office later that afternoon with an armful of flowers, I realized he begged to differ. His note read, "Last night was a dream, one I hope to keep having. Love, David."

He went back to Mississippi the next day, after a somewhat hopeful, mostly sad, good-bye. We spoke on the phone a few times after that before simply moving on. I, to not-great prospects.

In fact, I was no longer psyched to be single and found myself weighing my imaginary options between a life down South and a future as an expat's wife. Then, on the sixth-month anniversary of our breakup, William called.

He was in town on business and wanted to know if I would like to meet him for dinner. It was a sign. I said yes.

We decided to meet at his parents' Soho loft. I would go up for a drink with them at 7:00 P.M., he would come and buzz at 7:30 P.M., as he couldn't bear to face me and them in the same room. While I was not sure if I truly missed William, I knew that I missed his mother and father. They had always been kind and generous and had made me feel part of their family. She was an artist and beautiful, he a liberal—with a huge inheritance—who worked in education. Just before William and I had broken up, his mother had worriedly asked me what had happened to her activist son.

When the elevator opened into their apartment, William's parents were waiting for me with open arms. They missed me too, they said, and she ushered me into the living room as he poured me a glass of wine. We sat and caught up, but I noticed the strain. She was nervous, which made him irritable and then bossy. I had a future flash: me nervous, William bossy—and then the buzzer rang.

I kissed William's parents good-bye and rode the elevator down four flights, sensing that once the doors opened, I would know in an instant whether William was my man. The elevator landed with a thump, and there he stood, alone in the small lobby, dressed in a double-breasted raincoat. His black leather briefcase was clasped tightly in one hand. He was pale and shiny from a thin coat of sweat and had the panicky look of desperation in his eyes. Suddenly, I was single again.

parlors
and
ports

travel love

eva amy sohn

A long time ago, when I was having problems with an over-therapized boyfriend, I found myself wishing I'd been born in Victorian England. My boyfriend was complaining that he couldn't tell me he loved me because of his relationship with his mother, and that he couldn't sleep over because of the toll it took on his energy level, and I thought, In the old days guys weren't such whiners. They did what was required of them. They didn't just say "I love you," they brought you flowers and kissed your hand and killed themselves if you wouldn't have them.

But back in Victorian England you had to marry if you wanted to eat, your life span was about thirty years, and if you caught a cold you'd be dead in a week. So I knew there were some advantages to the modern single life. And in fact, it turned out that my boyfriend's trouble with "I love you" *was* a sign that something was wrong, and we both realized the relationship wasn't working and broke up soon after. But as hard as I tried to adapt to modern times, I never stopped feeling like I'd been born in the wrong era.

I'd go out and meet a guy at a party, and we'd hit it off, and the next day I'd send him a three-page letter about the incredible depth of my affection. Or, after one pretty good date, I'd try to think of the perfect gift, spend hours hunting it down, and deliver it personally to his door. I kept hoping one of the guys would turn out to be wrong-era too, and not only appreciate my obsolete romantic spirit but fall in love with me because of it. Instead they all freaked out and blew me off.

Then I met a guy named Ethan Allen. We met at that hipster swingers' bar, the one that's always open and has branches all over the country: a film festival. The festival was in a beach town, so we would lie on the sand and stare at the sky and make out and hold each other till the sun rose. It was like a honeymoon vacation, all expenses paid.

After three blissful days together the festival ended, and we went our separate ways—he to northern New York, I to southern—and by necessity, I was catapulted into the life of a Victorian heroine, with long, poetic correspondences, weeks between visits, and tortured declarations of longing. There were emails and phone calls, and sparse weekend meetings, and even though he was only a short hop from the city, in my mind he was on the battlefront and I was pregnant with our unborn child, counting down the days till I saw him next.

The first time I called him, I mentioned that I was lying on the bed. When you mention that you're lying on the bed, you'd better be prepared for what happens next. One thing led to another, and before I knew it we were practicing the quite un-Victorian art of P.S.-ing—phone-sexing.

The P.S. started out textbook delicious, but about a half hour in I found myself confronted with a terrible case of U.A., urination anxiety. I had really bad U.A., P.S.-inhibiting U.A., and knew I had it, but what could I say? You can't pee in front of a guy before you even go on date one. I kept talking and rubbing and hoping I'd just pee when I came and it wouldn't matter, I'd clean the sheets; but nothing was doing.

Just as I was beginning to despair, I heard this running water noise on his end of the line. "What's that?" I said.

"I'm peeing," he said. "I hope you don't mind."

"Not at all!" I screamed. "Now I can too!"

He laughed, and I ran into the bathroom and went and then I got back into bed. I told him I wanted him to come first, and he did. And then I knew I was going to, but I was nervous. So I said, "I'm going to put the phone down for a bit and you won't hear anything for a while, but then I'll pick it up again and you will."

"All right," he said.

I set the receiver on the pillow and kept going, and four or five minutes later I picked it up to tell him. "I'm coming!" I shouted. He didn't say anything, which I found surprising, and then I realized I'd picked up the phone wrong. The mouth was in my ear and the ear was in my mouth. I flipped it around and said, "Hello? Hello?"

"Yes?"

"I SAID I'M COMING!" I repeated joyously, and he moaned along with me, and that was our Very First Time.

It was strange to have P.S. before we had real sex, but there is an intimacy to phone sex that's hard to approximate in bed— it's verbal and revealing and creative. You feel like you know the person, and at the end you feel more close instead of less, and you don't have to lie there feeling vulnerable as he gets up to get something to eat.

After the P.S. came more P.S., and progressively steamier e-pistles, and agonizingly long, late-night phone talks. He'd call to tell me what the moon looked like out his window and I'd look out and try to see it from mine, which wasn't very easy since I lived in a street-level apartment. Other times I'd ask him to describe the layout of the cabin he was living in, and he'd ask me if I was wearing a fancy bra or un-glam Minimizer.

Although he often lamented that we were so far apart, there was a part of me that didn't want to trade in what we had. If we were both in New York City, and caught up in the drama of urban life, we'd never have the luxury of long phone conversations and we'd never want to spend the time sending detailed, mulled-over messages. And if we were together all the time, we might get sick of each other and eventually we might not have so many romantic thoughts about each other at all.

As much as I loved the P.S. and e-pistles, though, the best part of the distance was the visits. There is nothing like riding a train on the way to see someone you love. Imagine the heart-skipping feeling on the way to a third date with someone you like and multiply the palpitations by a thousand.

For my first visit he invited me to spend the weekend with

him, and the day I left was so sweltering that I had to take two showers not to smell. I put a dab of White Musk behind each ear, and around my neck I hung a white-and-blue puka shell necklace I'd been wearing all summer. I shaved my pubes to make a really neat triangle and went down the street to the Korean woman who waxes my mustache, and when I got home I dressed in this 1940s flowery high-waisted dress I bought at the Village Scandal. It fit me perfectly and reminded me of what women used to wear on trains back in the day when everyone dressed up to ride the trains. I packed my bag full of overnight clothes and a tank top to sleep in, a tank top that made me feel like a centerfold, and my novel, because he wanted to read it, and four condoms, which I thought was cautious but not overoptimistic.

When I got on the train I sat by the window, and for the first hour I just read and spaced out and looked at the greenery. Before I knew it we were twenty minutes from his town and I got choked up and sweaty. I kept seeing myself bounding down the platform toward him, and my heart and throat got tight. I felt like it had been years since we'd seen each other, instead of weeks, and I wanted to fast-forward to the moment of our hello. But even as I wanted to fast-forward to it, I also wanted to postpone it as long as I could so I could be staring out the window, filled with expectation, for the whole long rest of my life.

The conductor announced my stop, and then he walked down the aisle and took the seat tag from the luggage rack above me. I pressed my face to the glass to look for the platform and straightened the creases in my skirt. The train started to slow, and I reached up for my bag and moved to the door. All the other people getting off at the stop were middle-aged hippies, and I wondered who was waiting for them, how often they took this same train, whether I'd see their faces again the next time.

As we pulled into the station, I looked out the window and saw him looking away, down the platform, expecting me to dismount from somewhere else. He seemed anxious, which made me relieved. I didn't want him to be cool and collected. I wanted him to be as nervous as I was.

My door opened and the conductor hopped off and put a yellow stool under the bottom step. A man got out in front of me, and then I did. Ethan was right smack in front of me, leaning against a pillar, and I bounded down the stairs as fast as I could and barreled into his arms.

"Hi," he said, and I kissed him hard and sweet, and we stood there for a long time embracing and sighing. All the people who'd gotten off with me were greeting their lovers too, and I felt like we were all in cahoots, playing this mysterious, tantalizing game of travel love.

When we got to Ethan's car, he opened the door for me and mauled me for a while in the seat, and then he went around to his side. I leaned over to open the lock like Kyra Sedgwick does for Campbell Scott in *Singles,* but it was automatic and already up so I didn't have to. He noticed that I'd made the effort, though, and said, "You tried to open my door. That's a very good sign."

"I know it is," I said.

He turned on the engine, and as soon as we got on the road he pulled my knee close to his. He pushed up the skirt a little so the knee was out, and he squeezed it softly. I don't have great knees, they're bulbous and slightly bruised, but the flower pattern looked good against the tan of my skin. He held on to that knee almost every second of the half hour drive to his place, and much later when I got back home I could still feel the imprint of his hand.

in translation

~ julianna baggott

American men are emotional box turtles. Now, I like a nice box turtle. I had one as a child and scrubbed its shell with a specified toothbrush. And I could have spent my life, without interruption, coaxing my countrymen out of their shells with turtle food and scrubbing their tough backs. But when I was twenty I had a taste of something different. I went to Europe, where I realized that European men aren't box turtles. (There may be certain European exclusions—the British, for example, hustling in their tweed or galumphing in combat boots and blue hair.) But in general, I realized, European men are big slobbering farm dogs of love—great, happy, howling, shameless, tongue-hanging, leg-humping, too-big-to-be-in-your-lap-but-there-they-are-anyway dogs.

I was visiting the City of Love under the ridiculous but fabulous guise of "foreign exchange student," spending time in smoke-filled bars wearing liquid eyeliner and a leather bolero jacket with twenty-some zippers. I had this Janet Jackson layered look and a don't-slap-me-cause-I'm-not-in-the-mood, Miss-Baggott-if-you're-nasty stare. But I was a sweetheart, really, like one of those cookies with the soft cherry center. And part of the reason I'm telling this story as opposed to one that came later is that being free to do what you want when you want to is much less interesting than being freed, for the first time. I had the overwhelming feeling of having been let loose, unboxed.

At first I was in love with Paris itself. For a week or two, I ran almost everywhere I went. I showed up breathless so often that I was asked more than once if I was asthmatic. This is how it was, or at least how I remember it: men and boys, winking, smiling, waving, cheering, chanting—did they chant? It was like a glorious homecoming for me, a scrawny American who'd only been liberated a few years earlier from Catholic high school and my green herringbone miniskirt (too short to be regulation, but fuck it) and my polyester blazer, which I refused to wear in the halls even when it meant detention. I was finally appreciated, with an extravagance of scorching stares, flowers, an overwhelming, constant, boundless doggy lust.

Eventually, however, I realized that it wasn't only my glorious presence that inspired reticent hearts to soar. These hearts soared pretty easily, regularly, in minute-to-minute kinds of ways, like homemade rocket-launcher kits. Flirtation mandatory. Gushing high art. Love an epidemic. French women were immune. I'd been mistaken, taking it personally.

After this new understanding, Paris wore me down. It toughened into a real city all around me. The elderly couple I lived with detested me. Their baby, a twenty-three-year-old playboy, still lived at home and occasionally dressed as some mascot—a squirrel?—to do promotions in grocery stores. Had he wanted to be an actor? Nothing was clear, because they didn't speak to me. Like a stinky sock pinched and held far away from the body, my room was at the end of a long, bent hallway, and I was encouraged to go straight there upon entering the house.

And although the French were still tirelessly romantic—my housemother had given me a tacky beige vase for the random roses given to me in restaurants, on the metro, in long white boxes sent to the house—I'd learned enough to tell the difference between a gaze and a leer, and the leers were exhausting. Plus, Frenchmen didn't like the fact that I was American. They often couldn't place my accent, but when I placed it for them, they'd say things like, "I find most American women are fat and stupid as cows." So I spent more time than I'd expected giving them the finger, telling them to fuck off, throwing drinks and whatnot.

And so I felt alone, single in a way that I hadn't ever been before. The feeling of being let loose felt more like uprooted, untethered, floating. This is the mood I was in one night when I was hanging out with my best friend, Elise, also an exchange student, who was living on the East Side in Chinatown. A gorgeous genius, she'd popped up, inexplicably, from the soil of Cumberland, Maryland, but she was odd in a worldly way. She was a giant-eyed blonde wearing a leather jacket she'd spotted on the metro tracks and had climbed down to claim. On this night she'd walked up to the bar, ordered something ridiculously beyond her years, like a Dewars straight-up. She'd asked the guy next to her for a cigarette, lit up, and addressed the men in general, "Who has a yacht? Who would like to take me to Greece?"

It so happened that there was a Brit, a rich guy, a little older than her father, who said he'd be happy to take her to Greece, and so we ran up his tab and smoked his cigarettes. I got bored, wandered off. And this is all I know: T. was in a corner booth with a crowd of guys, and then, I'm not sure how it came to be, I was sitting next to him, his arm wrapped around me, our faces an inch apart. His English was shoddy and my French was improving, jumbled but fast. Did T. and I kiss in the bar? On the street? Did Elise drag me away to catch the last metro, where we sat dazed and dreamy till our subway lines split? Probably yes to all of that.

All that freedom had made me weary, and so I did the most logical thing with it—I handed some of it back. I fell in love with a Frenchman, and he was the perfect Frenchman to fall in love with, because he was about to be shipped off to Antarctica for fourteen months to do mandatory military service. It's not every day that you meet someone who's about to be shipped off to Antarctica, French or not. That's one of the points here. And when you do meet a Frenchman about to be shipped off (he actually took a flight out, but "shipped off" sounds so much more romantic), you should take full advantage of it. It's a fabulous story line. It promises weepingly orgasmic sex. The breathless, grief-stricken airport scene is a foregone conclusion. There will be months where you can languish painfully, wandering around a wounded romantic; and there's always the hope of a torrid reunion.

T. lived in the north of Paris near a fish market. We did a few datelike things, but mostly we lazed in a cot in the blue kitchen of his tiny apartment. I remember high, small windows that poured blue light. It was getting cold, and the heat purred weakly only every once in a while. The shower and the sink were miniature, like so many things in France, as if all midgets there are encouraged to become architects, elevator and appliance designers. I became an ambassador of sorts, explaining American culture. He was most interested in song lyrics. I did the best I could but may have taught him that "Tramps like us" was "Tram slap Gus." Why? he wanted to know. I was patient. It doesn't mean anything. It just sounds good. It's artistic. We had sex, slow and bluesy. It didn't have any of the rush, rush, gimmee, gimmee feel of other sex I'd had. In fact he was the perfect mix of my great, bounding St. Bernard impression of European men and the American box turtles I was comfortable with back home. He had beautiful soft lips and sweet blue eyes. And I loved him, didn't I?

For a while, I spent my days in class, learning French through muffled earphones, exact replicas of the ones in the U.S. It was like if the Franklin Institute had decided to build its version of a rain forest in a rain forest instead of in Philadelphia. Was I the only one to realize that learning French culture in a classroom while in the real France was idiotic? It was an irony that I found unbearable. I was a devotee of irony early on. In one class, when asked for a synonym for disgusting, I raised my hand and offered a dirty word, not knowing it was a dirty word, just proud. The teacher stiffened.

"You did not learn that word at le Sorbonne!" And I thought, Oh, you're right. I learned that in a bar near le Sorbonne. Soon enough I stopped going to classes altogether.

Of course, it wasn't only the irony that drove me off. There was another reason. I preferred spending time with T., and it was slipping fast. He wanted me to meet his family, and so one night we took a train to a small fishing town on the west coast. The house was small and damp, with a large vegetable garden that took up the backyard. There was a big family dinner at a long table set up in the middle of the living room. His sisters looked medieval—black hair, red faces, bulbous noses, even on the pudgy, adoring little sister. His mother was a flushed, busty woman in a flower-print dress. And there was a bunch of ruddy uncles—all fishermen. Even though I spoke French well enough, they didn't speak to me directly. They treated me like abstract art, like something their boy had made himself—out of leather and zippers and liquid eyeliner—in an art class in the big city, something you'd put on the mantel and try to ignore as best you could. They did offer me cigarettes because, they told me, all Americans smoke. I tried to explain that there was a fitness craze in the States, but I was met with blank stares. His mother, confused by it all, petted me, which I took as a signal to stop talking. After I accidentally locked myself in the bathroom during the dinner party and had to knock and knock to get their attention to let me out, T.'s mother made one of the uncles fix the doorknob, although there was nothing wrong with it aside from it being backward from mine at home.

What was clear most of all was that the relationship wasn't going to end when he got on the plane. I was in deep now, and,

I think, blindly, happily so. We went to bon voyage South Pole parties. And the day came. Weepy orgasmic sex. The airport scene. Do I have to go through it? You know what I'm getting at, story line. And that was part of it. Wasn't I just being dramatic, trying to live a grand, sweeping plotline? I'd wanted to be a writer since I was nine, and I'd heard that writers really had to live to be able to write (probably some ultra-male Hemingway notion); and I felt like I was doing what I was supposed to be doing—not as a girl wearing my school-badge blazer, but as a writer.

After a dismal Christmas with two friends in the pimp district of Rome, where we saved our money to buy a chocolate display cake that must have been two months old, I ended up at home back in Philadelphia. For a few days, I found myself mentally pointing out Americans—something that had become a habit. Backpacks, baseball caps, Nikes. But soon I caught on. It took a month or two before I lost the liquid eyeliner and didn't replace it. And eventually it got too hot for the bolero jacket, which went to the back of the closet. I knew it wouldn't resurface.

This was all pre-email. Once the ice stopped the mail ships, T. and I faxed. Phone calls were ten dollars a minute. When the ice thawed, there were boxes of letters that arrived day after day. There were photographs of penguins, sure, and occasionally, the story of somebody losing a toe, part of a hand, but mostly they were gorgeous love letters. He was going to get out in February. I took extra classes through the summer and fall and graduated early. I met him at an airport in New Jersey.

And what had worked in France didn't translate here. My

parents were a little giddy, which is how they get around foreigners. They trotted out their clunky French: *"Bon-jour!"* and *"Passez du beurre, s'il vous plaît!"* We visited my friends, still in college, and T. looked alternately blindsided and bored. He drank coffee and smoked cigarettes and acted French, which had worked so well in France but fell flat here. This was post La Yogurt and Le Car, but well before America flocked to coffee bars and college kids took up smoking again and, in general, entertained the idea of trying to appear more bourgeois Euro. I realized that I'd needed him in Paris, and here he needed me. The shift in power didn't work. We flew to Florida and fell apart. We flew back. The next day I drove him to a bus station. He got on a bus.

I went back to Paris last year. My novel *Girl Talk* came out in French under the title *Comme Elle Respire,* and I'd badgered my agent to tell the French editor that I was fluent, which wasn't a complete lie since I had been, once upon a time, ten or so years before. My editor asked to have me over. I was married by this point, and it was strange to be returning with my husband to this hazy, blue, floaty place that had come to symbolize the time in my life when I was first really free. In the weeks before the trip, I started dreaming about seeing T. on the street. Sometimes in the dream I would call out, but more often I'd follow him for a block or two, watch him dodge traffic, buy a newspaper. It was an ache, not guilt so much as the feeling that something that had been wrapped was now unwrapped, sifted, left open and rifled through. Of course I knew that I wouldn't bump into him. He'd never really loved Paris. Its bustle didn't suit him. (He'd actually liked Antarctica.) Still, instead of boning up for French interviews, I tried to work out just what I might say to T. if I met him on the street. It seemed essential to have that worked out, but nothing came to me.

Once in Paris, I concentrated on the pressures at hand. I'm so embarrassingly in love with my husband that I didn't particularly notice the Frenchmen gawking, or perhaps they'd stopped. Either way, it was different. I was focused and unaware. And I wasn't as haunted by thoughts of T. as I'd thought I would be. Until I was put on a panel on LCI, their version of CNN. Sophie Marceau, a former Bond girl, the Julia Roberts of France, sat beside me. I didn't know her. I kept asking her what she'd written, and she kept saying that she was Sophie Marceau. It meant nothing. Yes, but what's the title of your book? I kept telling myself not to be nervous, that it wasn't like doing an interview in English. No one would ever see this tape at home. And I had that rush of freedom again.

The hostess started up with me first. I could tell that she was summarizing my novel, and then at the very end she mentioned the mythologically large penis featured in it. She handed the question to me. But I didn't catch the question. Had there been a question? That twenty-year-old bubbled to the surface. I didn't know anybody out there listening to this. Everyone I knew was just waking up, having breakfast, flipping through the news of my own country. I didn't have much time to think. I blurted in French, "Ah, the big dick," and went on to say it was a Marquezian influence and that James Elroy and I had the same agent; I'd been told to say that; the French love Elroy. I blathered, blithely, then stared, big-eyed, at the interviewer. I could hear my old French professor: "She didn't learn that word at le Sorbonne!" And now I remembered what it was like sitting at T.'s family's long dinner table, with my painted eyes, my bolero jacket. Did the interviewer want to pet me, like T.'s mother, to make me stop talking? I thought of T.'s whole family, his medieval sisters, his fishing uncles.

Especially T. himself. I pictured him clearly, a man in some other kitchen now his own, still blue-eyed, still soft-mouthed, and he existed in a way he hadn't for years. He seemed so real, so ordinary, standing beside a miniature sink. I didn't really care what he thought, but I hoped he'd seen me there, fleetingly, before the camera beamed its love on Sophie Marceau, who didn't say "big dick" and was Frenchly, stoically unmoved that I had. I needed him again, and this image of him arrived. Maybe the relationship had been more about comfort than drama, after all.

T. seemed so real suddenly that I wanted to ask him about the old kitchen with its soft cot. If he ever thought of those stretched hours we spent together, and did he remember that the light was always blue? Would he agree? And I knew that's what I'd say. The kitchen was so blue, and why was that?

how to be alone

ⁿ⁰ lisa gabriele

P erhaps it is fate.

It is fall, 2001. The towers have fallen in a city you love. George is this adorable guy who happens to be sitting next to you in a bar in Greenwich Village. He is leaving for California the next morning, for five months of snowboarding and God knows what else. Weird, but you have so much in common: You both cut your orange juice with water. You both love Maugham. You're both from big families.

George is leaving early and so declines your invitation to join you and your friend at another bar in Soho. "Alas," you say, "such bad timing. We only just met, but I feel I've known you my whole life." You laugh at the cliché. "Yeah," he says, "and what if you're, like, the One." And you shrug and say,

"Yeah, well, what if?" You part, dropping a look that says you have known him your whole life.

You long for him in the cab in a way that cracks your friend up. She thinks you're kidding. After all, he's just some guy you met in a bar. So what that you gave him your email address. He'll never write. You'll never see him again. But you feel sorely deflated at the next bar, stupidly missing this George guy, who reads Maugham and seemed so sad and happy at the same time.

When someone taps you on the shoulder at Pravda, you turn around, irritated. It takes you a minute to recognize George in his wool hat, his cab idling outside. He says he came across town to kiss you good-bye. You scream and throw your arms around him. You kiss in a way that makes the bar erupt in applause. He says he'll write. You say you will, too. He leaves. You are imaginarily in love. Again.

Perhaps it is genetic.

It is 1976. Your younger brother, Sean, has an imaginary friend called the Little Bear. The Little Bear goes everywhere with Sean. It eats next to him at the dining room table and sits in the backseat of the red station wagon, your mother forcing the rest of you to clear a teeny space between you. When you aren't in a venal mood, you, your other brother, and your sister ask Sean about his friend. What does he look like? Oh. And how big is he? How old is he? And then you snicker. You are eight and don't feel much like making space for the Little Bear during a long road trip.

Sean shrugs and says, "I no care. Him gonna hoed da winnow."

"He's going to hold on to the window? With his little fingers?" you ask.

"Yah," Sean whispers, conspiratorially. "See? Him gonna float outsigh."

He smiles and waves and nods at his imaginary friend.

"Aww, how cute," you say, and then to Sean's mounting horror, you slowly roll up the window on the Little Bear's imaginary paws, holding on for his imaginary life. Sean screams, primally. Your mother pulls over, reaches back and rolls down the window. She smacks your murderous hands.

"There, see, he's saved. See?" she says to Sean, glaring at you. He wraps his arms around a bucket of air and stops sobbing.

Later your mother scolds you.

"Never, never do that! That bear is as real to Sean as we are to him," she explains.

"That's stupid. If we can't see him, how can he be real?"

"Because Sean believes he's real. That's how love works sometimes."

"Oh."

About a year later, the Little Bear disappears. When you ask Sean about his imaginary friend he tilts his head and says, "He go away. Poof. Gone."

Perhaps it is psychological.

It is 1977. Your dad leaves but returns after two months. No one says anything. Then he leaves for six months, for work out West. Then he returns. Everyone says everything. Then he leaves because he can't stand the sound of everyone saying everything, and he spends a year on your nona's couch. You don't tell your friends, since all their fathers seem as permanent as the pavement on their driveways. Besides, he always comes back. When your dad returns from Nona's, you follow him around the house, scaring him in the kitchen and garage like a little, needy ghost.

"Jeez! You scared me! What are you doing there?" he says.

"Nothing," you say, coming out from under the table or inside the closet.

A counselor from the church begins a weekly family therapy session in your living room. You fill out a questionnaire about how it feels to hear your parents fight. You circle *bad*, hard, in your Catholic Marriage Encounter Workbook for Kids. You color the little girl in the margin, giving her blue hair and red eyes. She is holding a teddy bear. You gently crayon it brown. You show Sean. He smiles.

After a big fight about his "necessity for self-actualization," your dad leaves for good, to find himself. You want to poke him through the middle with your finger and say, "But you're right here, I can see you." Instead, you begin keeping a diary, and a vigil. You are a girl with a perpetual candle burning in her window, hugging a bucket of air.

Perhaps it is circumstantial.

It is summer, 1983. Though you all go to Huronia Hockey Camp, it's meant for your brothers, your mother says. They need to be around men, though it has been a while since you've smelled Speed Stick or Brut or steak. All those dads yelling and sons sweating make you and your sister feel like you are swimming in Good Man Soup. Yay!

Kurt, a forward from Kenora, gives you your first French

kiss. You let him see you cry, once, and in your diary you describe him as "my one and only totally true love." Two weeks of sighs and promises, and you say good-bye in a flourish of exchanged addresses and phone numbers, and plans for a major future together. The first long-distance call is so intoxicating that you can't remember things to tell him. You are thinking, He called, he called, he is talking to you from far away. Then he stops calling, for no good reason that his mother can imagine. And, no he hasn't mentioned anything about you, no, not that his mother can recall.

You make up conversations in your diary, under the heading, "This Really Happened!!!" You read it aloud to your sister Sue.

Kurt says: *"It's going to be very hard to make our love work, but I don't care what it takes or how hard it's going to be for us to be together, but we will be together, forever, I swear. To hell with anyone that wants to keep us apart from each other. I won't stand for it. I love you too much and I miss you so much it hurts like hell to be so far away from you, your one true love in the world 'til I die."*

He is fourteen when you grant him these words.

"Wow, he really loves you," Sue exclaims. "What are you going to do?"

"I don't know. It's going to be really hard, like he says, you know? But our love is strong," you say.

"Totally strong," says Sue.

"Me and Kurt will be together again."

"Totally."

Your New Year's Resolution for 1984 is to get over Kurt.

Your New Year's Resolution for 1985 is to get over Kurt.

Perhaps it is accidental.

It is 1986. You are introduced to Mark at his going-away party. He is leaving for Texas, to train for a professional football career. A slow dance is followed by a heavy petting session, which culminates in a long, weepy kiss at the Detroit Metro airport. You are almost eighteen and not allowed to move out of the house until your birthday. After months of phone calls and treacly Hallmarks, you board a flight to Dallas, to blow out candles with your new man.

Mark greets you kindly at the airport, sweetly shows you your room, and then he shows you his, which has an antique tin ceiling, one which you spend a lot of time getting to know. Mark is the first man who has ever gone down on you. Holy. Fucking. Christ. Getting your pussy licked by a champ is like finding God, doing coke, and being a billionaire, all at the same time. You can never look back.

After a while, your mother stops accepting most of your collect calls. When she does let you through, you use a new kind of voice, the high, lying kind, to hide your boredom and regret. Because though coming and coming and coming is amazing, being with Mark is not as fun as missing him. It is duller, and fraught with difficulty. What will happen if he smells your farts? Or sees the stretch marks at the tops of your thighs? What if his bad breath is not something that only afflicts him in the morning? Waiting for him to come home all day is much harder than missing him from afar was.

"Why are you there? Why are you being so stupid?" your mom says.

"I'm not being stupid, I'm having a damn adventure!" you say.

Your sister, Sue, still lives at home, coaching soccer for a retarded kids league. She is qualified to negotiate the growing space between you and your mother.

"She's just having an adventure, Ma," Sue says, on the extension.

"Adventure, my ass. You have to get over Dad leaving, or you'll be following these guys around your whole entire life." Click. *Banhhhhhh.*

It's time to leave Texas, and you cry at the airport, embarrassingly, and a lot. Mark calls when you get home. You have six or seven more conversations. But without his tongue on your pussy, you find it hard to make your own tongue form useful conversation. You are accepted to a faraway university and forget about the girl back in Texas, flat on her back, knees slack, seeing fireworks in the patterns in the tin roof of a rented bungalow.

Perhaps it's unavoidable.

It is 1987. On your first date, Carey grabs a hard fistful of your permed hair and kisses your Bonne Belle mouth. He has the spoiled face of rich kids, those who have judges for dads, who notice that yours isn't around anymore. On your second date, he puts your hand on the outside of his stiff Dockers and says, "Feel that? That's your fault. Now tell me what you're gonna do about it, missy?"

"This is what I'm going to do about it," you say, your face

like the sun setting down the front of his Lacoste shirt. You give him the kind of blow job that makes him whelp like he just got born.

On your third date, dinner at your place, he presents you with a bottle of champagne. His fingers are sticky from you, so you do the honors. Seems he has been accepted into law school, locally. He toasts the fact that you are accepted at a far-away university to major in painting and drawing, or as Sue says, "pining and bawling." You place your hand on his hand and promise him that you will try to come home at least twice a month, and that he will visit as often.

"So we'll just see each other on the weekends, and then in the summers I'll move home, and then maybe you can get a transfer to the law school at my university, if you can get your marks up, because obviously you wouldn't want to stay—"

Carey interrupts.

"Um, I like you a lot. I really do. But why should we bother? You're leaving."

"Why bother? Why BOTHER! What if we fall in love?" you say, though you'd like to add, Because my breath smells like you, and your hands smell like me, is why we should bother!

Carey says, "Falling in love won't happen if we don't see each other anymore. It's unhealthy for us to start something knowing we aren't going to be together. Let's just have fun tonight, and see what happens down the line!"

Then he takes out his penis, which stiffens in your hand. You look at it for a second, then drop it like a phone when the line's gone dead.

*   *   *

Perhaps it is recreational.

It is 1995. In Havana, Cuba, with college friends, you spot Guillermo from across a crowded salsa club. You dance dirty and well together, spend the night cuddling, and he leaves for Argentina the next morning. When you receive his FedEx, stuffed with an eight-page letter written in Spanish and a mixed tape of Argentinean rock and roll (gay), and a photo taken on the plane, his face frowning, the back inscribed with "Te estrano, ya" (sweet), you imagine babies with brown arms and an overweight, benevolent mother-in-law. After six months of expensive calls and cheap tears, because after all, you hardly understand a word he says, he tells you he is coming to visit. You pick him up at the airport, feeling nauseous and uncertain. He seems smaller. His English is better, though he remarks that your pigtails make you look like a little "neeger." This must be a misunderstanding, because your best friend, a black lesbian, is to be the first to meet him. When you explain you'll be catching up with her at the Gay Pride Parade that afternoon, Guille rolls his eyes in an impatient way.

Before you leave a note that says, "*Guille, I'm at my brother's. Please leave my apartment by the time I get back. This will not work out.*" And before he replies, "*Fine. I find it cold in so many times here. You are very bored to me. I can't see your face again, because it make me sic* (sic)." Before all that, he has said to you, "Homosexuality ees abhorrente ee unnaturale, no? And she ees negro? I am no good wi' dizz."

How did you not know this about him? How did you not know that he is a racist homophobe? Oh, right, you had never really met him before.

*   *   *

Perhaps it is perennial.

It is summer 2002. You return to New York City after a winter of visiting George in California. You do, in fact, have a lot in common. A love of morning sex, cats, Cabernet, and a particular propensity toward long-distance relationships. You don't think that the latter might be the wrong thing to have in common, until he moves back to the City. You break up shortly after that. For months you date others, and so does he, often running into each other in the neighborhood. But it's no big deal, really.

But soon you two are meeting again, for casual drinks. Soon his tongue is back in your ear and elsewhere. Then you are lounging in your pajamas watching videos and playing backgammon, snickering at the awful movies you seem to pick to see. Why are you spending every other night together? What's the point of dating again? After all, he is leaving for California in three weeks, again, for five months of snowboarding and God knows what else. And you're not putting yourself through this again. No more phone calls and tears and pining. No more fucking and crying, often at the same time. You promise yourself that you will say a firm good-bye. You won't wait by the phone for his calls. You won't expect a visit, a commitment, a change of address, permanently together, forever always. No. When he goes, at first, he will be your Little Bear, and you will let him sit next to you on the subway, invisible and warm, and then he will forget to call on Valentine's Day, and you will let him float beside you, there, but not there. And then one day, he won't return your email, after which you will find it hard to find the time to visit, then he will meet someone at a bar in Truckee, and you will finally go out with that human rights lawyer everyone's always trying to set you up with. Then you will roll up the window on your imaginary boyfriend's fingers, all ten no doubt holding on but never as tight as you need him to be. Then poof. Then gone.

Or maybe not quite yet. Maybe you will pull him down into your lap, and he'll weigh more than air, and you will hold on until he appears real again, like a man sitting next to a woman, both heading in the same direction.

around the world
in 80 dates

୬ susan dominus

A month after I shoved my college diploma into a box and dolefully moved back home, one of my best friends moved to Thailand. Even now, when I hear about the nights she camped out with her boyfriend on the beaches of Shang Mai, or the days she staggered triumphantly to peaks of the Himalayas, I wonder with a wallop of regret why I didn't join her, if only for a few weeks. Then I remember, Oh right, too broke. I was broke for most of my twenties, not broke in a gnawing-hungry kind of way, just broke in the kind of way that meant an empty bottle of hair conditioner was an irritating budgetary setback. I did manage to find an apartment in New York, but after my share of the rent, there wasn't much cash left over for airfare out of town. In six years, I think I left the East Coast once, when an oil man flew me out to Jackson Hole to tutor his sulky daughter for a week.

But that wasn't travel—it didn't entail the scent of hibiscus, or pilgrimages to Great Art, or generous, startling invitations from unlikely sources. I was young and jumpy and expectant, stunned by the tedium of a job that entailed voluminous faxing and refaxing, followed by conversation after conversation about whether the fax had, in fact, arrived.

I longed for travel. I settled for dating. Or rather, I traveled through dating. Maybe I should have been looking for some nice boy who'd gone to school in New England, who wore a suit during the week, a baseball cap on weekends. Instead, I listened for accents, although I didn't know it at the time. My favorite belonged to Bunky, a corn-blue–eyed smoothie, so-named after his hometown (to me, mythical) in Louisiana. When he wanted a kiss, his eyes would go smoky and he'd say, "Come here and give me some sugar." Even *sugar* sounded sweeter out of his mouth—*shuguh*—with that open softness, much better than the hard, closed-off *grr* of the northeast. On weekends, we'd lie lazily in bed and he'd tell me about his friend's balcony in New Orleans, where he promised we'd sit and drink rum and Cokes during Mardi Gras, watching the crowd below until we'd had enough to drink to plunge in and lose ourselves. In the meantime, I let him take me to the Plaza Hotel, and we'd make out at the Oak Bar amid the smokelike strangers in a town we'd never set foot in again. I'm ashamed to say I made him dance the two-step with me at Denim N Diamonds, a Midtown club where Brooklyn boys hooted and hollered in ten-gallon hats. Bunky may have been Southern, but he didn't like the club. And yet he twirled and stomped with me gamely, precisely because he was Southern, and therefore old-fashioned, and therefore obliging. Also, after a few frozen margaritas, he'd do pretty much anything you asked.

Bunky and I parted ways when he started taking me to romantic restaurants with roses in vases—he was giving me the moonish looks of a sensitive guy, when I'd fallen for a sexy good ole boy. I was too skittish for that kind of serious languor, too curious about what or who came next. I was looking for adventure, and went directly to the source. The next man I dated was an Outward Bound instructor, a professional provider of adventure. He was apple-cheeked, goateed, fit, and handsome, alpha even on Rollerblades. He looked great in fleece, and we went hiking on weekends or stayed in town to catch this or that folksinger playing downtown. But there was a downside to my Outward Bound instructor's crunchy spirituality, which was that he wanted me to share it. We parted ways after he solemnly informed me my home was a cold place because it held no religious texts.

After that, my friends stopped keeping track. They listened indulgently, but they were particularly baffled by the haughty Milanese who read *Corriere della Sera* over scrambled eggs. His accent was more endearing than seductive—Italian, obviously, but with the British clipped *t*s he'd been taught at private school. He missed Italy, and I exploited that, trawling for details, until I could practically reminisce along with him about truffle hunting with friends in Tuscany, his mother's risotto ai funghi, the late Sunday Vespa rides speeding down an empty Via Tornabuoni. I couldn't head north for a ski weekend in the Alps, so I let the Alps come to me, in the form of a six-foot-three-inch warm-and-smooth–skinned law student. He emitted affection only occasionally, but atmosphere fairly reliably.

It wasn't so much that I needed to be physically transported; I simply needed enough vivid contrast to take me out of the here and now. At work, I'd graduated from full-time faxer to full-blown editor and accumulated a lively compendium of dating stories, but I still felt restless, unsatisfied—most of all, fearful. Instead of growing into my promotions, I felt a sense of defeat with each job change, as if I was exchanging carefree youth for prematurely high levels of professional responsibility. It's a measure of how lost I was at the time that I thought law school, of all things, might make me happier, and I went so far as to apply and then go. Looking back, I think I just wanted some time away from that inexorable walk to the subway every morning.

In truth, I didn't want to be a lawyer any more than I wanted to be an editor. I wanted to be a writer—a magazine writer, not such an outlandish dream, really—but nine thousand people had told me it couldn't be done, and I was the kind of person who figured nine thousand people couldn't be wrong. When I bailed out of law school after a year, I surprised myself by landing a job reporting throughout Europe. Even then, my fear of the unknown proved too great. I'd fought like hell for the job—then turned it down in favor of yet another editing gig back in New York.

I returned to my Midtown apartment in the city, where the inexorable walk to the subway resumed, as did the carousel of men. My roommate began to worry that I swapped personae depending on who I was dating—I'd suddenly be buying Memphis blues CDs, or sporting a Texas hipster suede jacket, or cooking a lot of Indian food. "It's like you don't know who you are," she'd say accusingly. I'd shrug: "You know the saying, When in Rome. . . ." I was confident I knew the way back, although she was right, all right: I had no idea who or where I was. Rather than face my here and now, I diverted myself in men's pasts, or went along for the ride as they wondered about their futures—as teachers living by a lake, as golf pros in the South, as globe-trotting early-retiree hedge fund managers. It was like being absorbed in the best travel writing. I lost myself in the specificity of their characters, soaking in the details of what writers call "color": their quirks, their cultural landmarks, the interplay of their unique failings and redeeming, miraculous virtues. I suppose I could have done the same thing with women, except that making briefly inseparable friendships is a harder trick than forging intense, if short-lived, romances. The world forgives a twenty-something who has no intention of marrying the men she dates. The world does not forgive a woman who seduces and drops friends, sometimes as many as two in a month, simply because she was curious and in need of a change of scenery.

I've always found it metaphorically compelling that we grow more shortsighted as we grow up, as if we lose, with age, the ability to project ourselves too far afield. In the best of all possible ways, I grew nearsighted as I approached thirty—I stopped trying to make sense of the mesmerizing blur of other people's lives (men, mostly), and started to focus on my own, on what lay directly in front of me. I started writing, first moonlighting, then full-time. Taking smaller risks emboldened me to take bigger ones, which led to opportunities for travel—at last, the long-delayed travel. I piled into jeeps with Eritrean soldiers, held my breath as a plane bore down sharply past the hills of Afghanistan to land in Kabul. On a flight back from Rome, the man next to me saw my Albania guidebook and guessed, correctly, that I'd come from there, where I'd been interviewing Kosovar refugees. "You're very brave," he said. I had to laugh, since at that very moment, I was clutching the arms of my seat, heart pounding, steeling myself for takeoff, as I do on every flight. I knew I wasn't brave, but simulating bravery seemed like a good first step.

Around the time my own life got more interesting, the men I dated became more familiar—friends of friends, old college classmates. At thirty, I met the man I would marry. He was not exotic; like me, he liked to go running and rent movies and read a lot. He knew a lot of people I knew. He was basically my age. My friends didn't call him "West Point Guy" or "Outward Bound Guy" or "Quaker Guy." They called him Alan. We fell in love.

It helped, of course, that he, too, was a writer and had also traveled widely, to Africa, Tasmania, Australia, for work. He was close to home, which meant he understood the need occasionally to leave it. Before we even got engaged, we began resurrecting an old dream of mine to move to the countryside of France (in college I'd turned down an opportunity to work at a cloister in Brittany). For seven months, we house-sat an oversized, half-furnished villa in southern Burgundy. We savor a lot of memories from that trip—the afternoon schnapps with our neighbors, the back garden's gluttonous offerings of apples and pears, the white cows blending into fall fog. And yet my sweetest memory may have formed before the trip officially began. As our plane left Kennedy airport for Lyon-Saint Exupéry, I felt a profound sense of relief—relief that I was finally traveling in the company of someone I knew well and trusted: me.

herland, revisited

ᴇᴠᴀ meghan daum

> The men may live in separate towns, or they may
> have subdued them somehow and keep them
> shut up. But there must be some.
>
> *Herland,* Charlotte Perkins Gilman, 1915

O f the several hundred times I have been asked what I
found to be the major cultural difference between New
York City, which I left in 1999, and Lincoln, Nebraska, where I
lived for the subsequent four years, I never once gave the truthful answer. It's hard to come across like an even semi-serious person when your chief intellectual assertion about New York
versus the Midwest has to do with male attention. But here you
have it: It wasn't tornadoes; it wasn't the astonishingly low cost of
living. It was the fact that in Lincoln I was overwhelmingly per-
ceived as an attractive, sexually desirable person, and, in New
York, my presence in, say, a bar teeming with testosterone-
charged twenty- and thirty-something males would have gone
virtually unnoticed—that is, if I could have found a bar teeming

with males of any age. This kind of dichotomy makes contrasts like weather and property taxes seem trivial.

There are few cultural observations that are less flattering to the observer and more apparently damaging to feminism than making note of what seems to be a grossly imbalanced gender ratio in New York City. It doesn't help that this imbalance is largely anecdotal, a mishmash of head counts made in restaurants and adult education classes, passing glances around the Laundromat, remembered statistics from magazines ("seven hundred thousand more single women than single men" is a quote that floats through my consciousness as though it were from *Hamlet,* though its origin is more mysterious than the Bard himself). The Census Bureau, though it does not keep track of marriage rates according to gender, did report in 2000 that there were 2,080,881 men and 2,563,986 women between the ages of twenty and forty-nine in New York City (in Lincoln these figures were 63,144 men and 59,014 women). That's not quite as wide a margin as the surplus of seven hundred thousand single women theory suggests, but, in my experience, if you ask women in New York where the men are, they're likely to point toward some netherworld over the rivers and into the distant woods.

Most of us are loathe to admit having any concerns in this area. We are not the kind of women who relate to the most readily available clichés about single womanhood—the punch lines about drowning sorrows in tubs of ice cream, the stare downs with the unringing telephone, the odd resiliency of the word *spinster.* Like most forms of mass-marketed neuroses, such platitudes are relegated to a place of kitsch. What is real, though, is the way a condition that at one time might have been characterized as spinsterhood has now become not only commonplace but also perhaps even the default in the city that is the largest in America and the fifth largest in the world. By that I mean that while we have more pressing things to do than waiting for phones to ring or consuming pints of Cherry Garcia in one sitting, we do find ourselves living in a place that reflects, if not an absence of men, a palpable underrepresentation of them. I am talking about the proliferation of tables at restaurants surrounded by five women and one or two men. I am talking about New York speed dating services who list their events as "closed to women" while male enrollment is barely at 50 percent. I am talking about the dinner parties in Brooklyn apartments attended by ten women wearing cargo pants and designer flip-flops, eating homemade lasagna and not exactly noticing that this is an all-female dinner party, just that it's a regular sort of gathering. I am talking about other dinner parties thrown by hostesses who scramble to find male guests to even out the room, only to wind up with the usual five-to-one ratio. Above all, I am talking about the fact that, now in my thirties, I barely notice anymore when a party or a café or a museum or a movie theater or even a street corner has women bursting from its seams and only a handful of men darting about like waiters in an understaffed restaurant. I read somewhere that the ratio of single women to single men on the Upper West Side of Manhattan was ten to one. Here again, I can see the statistic, typeface and all, but cannot find it in any archive (perhaps I dream these things). But the girls' dormitory—like the atmosphere of my last apartment building, on West Eighty-sixth Street—provides evidence enough, not because we were running around in our socks and nighties (we ranged in age from our twenties to our eighties and, like most New Yorkers, avoided eye contact in the elevator) but because the virtual nonexistence of men (save the handsome, young—and well-tipped—part-time doorman) was not an oddity but a matter of course.

Increasingly I am struck by how my particular experience of New York—and, to be sure, it's a minority experience, a world of educated (probably overly so) liberal arts types whose orbits are somewhat limited to publishing and media and yoga classes and any number of pursuits that arguably draw larger numbers of women than men (though I'm hard-pressed to characterize riding the Broadway IRT, which always seems to have more women, as a female activity)—resembles a world envisioned in the 1915 feminist Utopian novel *Herland,* in which author Charlotte Perkins Gilman imagined a civilization of women that had existed—in fact thrived—without men for two thousand years. Descended from a tribe of polygamous mountain people whose land closed in on itself after a series of natural disasters, the tribe resorted to infighting until "literally no one [was] left on this beautiful high garden but a bunch of hysterical girls and some slave women."[1] Over time, they created their own perfect society, even finding a way to reproduce themselves (only girl children) through a form of parthenogenesis. The result:

> *Their little country was quite safe. Their farms and gardens were all in full production. Such industries as they had were in careful order. The records of their past were all preserved, and for years the older women had*

---

1. *Herland* (Pantheon Books, 1979), p. 55.

*spent their time in the best teaching they were capable
of, that they might leave to the little group of sisters and
mothers all they possessed of skill and knowledge.*

There you have the start of Herland![2]

I do not confuse that description with anything approxi-
mating the culture of New York City—in Herland, inciden-
tally, "everything was beauty, order, perfect cleanness." But
the experience of leaving New York and coming back frequently for visits leaves me feeling a bit like *Herland*'s narrator, Van Jennings, one of three male explorers who stumble
into this strange land and slowly come to realize just how limited a definition of women the rest of the world (passingly re-
ferred to as "Ourland"[3]) is capable of offering. That's not to say
that women's lives in Lincoln have anything in common with
those of Victorian America—knapsack-toting college coeds
roam the streets in tank tops, a woman is currently mayor,
nearly everyone I knew over the age of thirty was either di-
vorced or openly gay or both—or that the women of New York
universally inhabit some higher plain of empowerment or au-
tonomy. It's just since I've been gone I have come to view this
legendary "man shortage" not as a cumbersome drawback to
living in New York but as a cornerstone of our very characters.

---

2. *Herland*, p. 57.
3. Praeger, 1997, p. 101. In 1916, Gilman published *With Her in Ourland,* a sequel to
Herland, in which Van Jennings takes his Herland bride, Ellador, into the real
world, where "she seemed more at a loss with the women than the men. . . . The
women were not so human; had a less wide outlook, less experience, as a rule.
When she did get near enough one of them for talk at all intimate, then came the
ultra-feminine point of view, the different sense of social and moral values, the peculiar limitations of their positions."

That's not something I could have wrapped my mind around while I lived in New York. Like a lot of women there, I was too busy being angry that I had to "compete" with so many women for so few men. But now that I've been away, now that I've left Herland for that great mass of Ourland, I am convinced that much of what makes the women of New York so fiercely funny and bright and unhesitant in their particular forms of world domination is that they live, if only on the level of dinner parties and certain apartment buildings, in a female-centric society. It may be what they hate most about New York. But since I left, it's what I miss the most.

When I lived in New York, I did not spend a lot of time thinking about the men and women of the city in terms of numbers. I just assumed I had a hard time meeting men, that I didn't get out enough, that when I did get out it was to go to lectures and art exhibits rather than Knicks games and paintball tournaments and, ergo, the snake was eating its tail and all of that. But when I moved to the Midwest, and, to a slightly lesser but not insignificant extent, when I moved to Los Angeles four years later, I was struck by how even the most incremental leveling of the gender ratio could affect the way people saw themselves and each other.[4] When I got to Lincoln, men seemed to be everywhere. There were men in supermarkets, men in libraries, men in coffee shops and pizza parlors

---

4. U.S. census data for men and women between the ages of 20 and 49 in the greater Los Angeles area show 2,229,899 men and 2,195,632 women.

And, in case you're interested, gender ratios for the same age groups in Chicago, Illinois, and Austin, Texas, break down as follows:

Chicago: 1,880,455 men versus 1,893,472 women

Austin: 338,942 men versus 312,679 women

Census Scope, Age Distribution by Sex, 2000: Los Angeles, Chicago, Austin–San Marcos; www.censusscope.org. Date retrieved 6/18/03.

and shopping malls and (I swear this is true, even in Nebraska) in Pilates classes. I got asked out more times during my first six months in Nebraska than I had during the entire eight years I'd lived in New York. At age thirty I experienced for the very first time what it meant to walk into a bar and have nearly every man look up and at least one or two offer to buy me a drink.

This is not because I was any more attractive than I had been in New York or that I was significantly more attractive than most women in Lincoln. Nor do I suspect it had much to do with being new in town or even being "open to new people," in the way that lifestyle gurus like to associate with changes of scene. I believe it is simply a matter of there being in Lincoln, Nebraska, relatively equal numbers of men and women, a demographic phenomenon that results in a reasonably attractive, unattached woman in a bar receiving male attention. When this demographic phenomenon does not exist, as is the case in New York, a woman ten times more attractive than I can walk into a bar and not get a second glance (data supplied by my ten-times-more-attractive friends and acquaintances). I am not suggesting that this is a problem of international crisis proportions, nor do I mean to imply that we couldn't use a few more places in this country where young women can walk into bars without any fanfare. What I do think is that it's time for the women of New York to realize that there are so many single women in the city because it's just about the best place on earth for us to be.

I say "us" because even though I no longer live in New York I will always remain, if not a New Yorker, a New York woman. Just about every important thing that ever happened to me happened in New York. It is where I was first paid to write, where

I first fell in love, where I first experienced both the rush of believing I really might get everything I ever wanted and the agony of wondering if I'd been a fool for harboring that belief. I will always be a New York woman because even after four years in Lincoln, where never-married, child-free women in their thirties are all but unheard of, I still had that myopic New York tendency to think of myself as squarely within the norm of American female life. It never occurred to me in Lincoln that a lot of people probably thought I was a lesbian. It took nearly four years to realize that the reason I did not enjoy dinner parties in Lincoln as much as I had in New York had less to do with the quality of the lasagna than with the fact that the women attending these parties, though they were delightful, smart, and compassionate, weren't exactly my kind of women. For all their intelligence and appealing eccentricities, their awareness of themselves as women had largely been formed in a way that is consistent with most American women's perceptions of themselves, which is that they know they share the world with equal numbers of men. In that world, men and women may or may not be equal, distribution of wealth and labor may or may not be fair, but men could always be counted on to provide, if nothing else, a reminder that they do indeed represent 49 percent of the American population.[5] For all the values and experiences these women and I had in common, none of them could have thrown an all-women dinner party without consciously planning it as an all-women event. Unless specified otherwise, men were just always around.

5. U.S. Census Bureau, Men and Women in the United States: Annual Demographic Supplement to the March 2002 Population Survey. Date retrieved 6/18/03.

This was a gulf between us that I eventually realized was unbridgeable. These women were not, to borrow Gilman's phrase, the "ultra-women" I knew from New York, the women who dressed fabulously whether men were around or not, the women whose reduced expectations for domestic bliss had opened the door for all kinds of other, more radical, expectations, the women for whom self-sufficiency was not a political act but a human function as natural as breathing. These are privileged states of being, to be sure. They are privileges that arise out of economics and region and individual personality traits and whatever millions of other variables contribute to the act of putting on a pair of Manolo Blahnik knockoffs in order to cook dinner in your apartment for your three best friends. Since I've been gone, I see that some of those privileges come from where we least expect them to. They come from that deficit of 483,105 men. They come from the spark we've misdiagnosed as frustration and the serenity we mistook for resignation. They come from Herland. I know because no matter how hard I look, I never quite find it in Ourland. I may have more dates, but they're at the cost of some pretty extraordinary dinner parties. Nothing in this life comes cheap.

allies
and
enemies

medusa's sister

✎ merrill markoe

It took me a long time to understand how even your basic sex act was performed. By the end of grade school, I had some interesting theories. From what I could tell, the penis pointed downward and the opening of the vagina went upward, so I figured maybe the way intercourse was achieved had something to do with having the woman standing on her head. When the actual logistics were finally explained, my grade-school friends were all very grossed out. "Eew." I remember one girl saying with a gargoyle-like grimace, "That is so disgusting. I wouldn't do that with my own father."

What I guess I am trying to say is that I was kind of naïve until I went off to college. My parents were terribly paranoid about the idea that I would be sexually active in any way. As a junior in high school, when my mother caught me in our backyard kissing my first boyfriend, she broke into hysterical tears. She was pushing the premise that any kind of one-on-one involvement with the opposite sex was bad for someone my age. "I don't want you to get emotionally involved," she said, confusing me even further by making emotions seem like a bigger problem than pregnancy or disease. On the bright side, my mother's version of the way things were supposed to work socially was a real piece of creative writing. She believed that there was a situation called "dating" that involved large groups of boys and girls gathered in brightly lit locations, unaware of the whole notion of two genders and with no particular interest in pairing off. Part of me knew that she was full of shit, yet another part of me felt that her terror must have a point. And so, despite my façade as a rebel hipster and budding artistic visionary, dressed only in black and always carrying a book of dark, violent poetry, I never really did much of anything in high school except burn incense and listen to Bob Dylan. By the time I graduated, I had only kissed two boys total and been felt up by one. I was still a virgin.

From the moment I got to college and became an art major I was in love with the poetry and tragedy that being an artist conferred on me. It gave me permission to be painfully conflicted in special, intriguing ways. Not only could I be as anorexic as I wanted, but now if I threatened to kill myself, I was taking with me a whole slate of never-to-be-realized masterpieces. Nice.

When I skulked around the long, echoing halls of the art department, I was no longer an insecure, identity-crisis–riddled, middle-class girl who was always on a diet. I was a dark, potentially brilliant, starving, Chekhovian creature: too sensitive and perceptive for your world.

As soon as I got the lay of the land, I tried to fine-tune the details of my new image in order to become an Important Artist in Training. Through careful data gathering, I was able to ascertain that the important artists of the late sixties dressed like ranch hands, drove trucks or motorcycles, and drank Jack Daniels straight up in dirty glasses. They rolled their own cigarettes with yellowed fingers and did artwork that involved the use of dangerous equipment, like acetylene torches and table saws. Like everything else that mattered, real art was a man's job. So as soon as I saved a little extra money, I bought a Black & Decker band saw, a power drill, and a belt sander. I was going to make sculpture, not because I liked to work in three dimensions but because of the amazing sense of macho competence I got from owning power tools. When I lit up a filterless Camel and turned on my band saw, I could feel my own sexual power for the first time. Maybe I couldn't work with a lit cigarette dangling from my lower lip, like I saw the important artists doing, without choking. But I had the will, and the desire. I would practice. Now I was a foot soldier in an important art war.

With my new power tools and some thigh-high leather boots, all that was really left to complete my new badass artistic identity was to get the fuck out of my all-girl dorm as quickly as possible. After a long day of macho posturing, an artist with power tools needed a studio, not a bunch of dorm bullshit. So when I succeeded, by dint of bad attitude, in getting myself thrown out, I was filled with glee. Now all I had to do was forge my parents' signatures on the appropriate forms and I was all set to move in to a live-in studio/storefront apartment some other students were vacating.

I could feel myself developing a new sexually magnetic invincibility. Despite the fact that my version of a ranch hand sometimes wore a miniskirt that came to the top of her thighs, I was nevertheless secure in the knowledge that my new tool-related competence had allowed me to effectively bypass every limitation and stereotype associated with my gender. And what bigger piece of validation did I need than the fact that my Internationally Famous art professor had begun to show special interest in me. Everyone wanted to study with him. But I was the one he wanted to talk to in his office after class. I sensed that he sensed the serious nature of my artistic intentions. He knew I was someone destined for greatness. I was thrilled.

As I told him about some of the things I was working on, I let him know that I was planning to take his class again summer quarter. He said it was an excellent idea. And then he gave me a thick pornographic novel, full of vivid descriptions of sexual acts. I had never read anything this graphic before. And at first I wasn't sure why he had given it to me. But the more I thought about it, the more I concluded that he knew it was important for me to broaden my narrow view of the world in the interest of becoming a better artist.

When I first brought up the idea of attending summer school, my parents looked at me like I was crazy. But I whined and begged and pleaded, and eventually I was able to talk them into letting me stay in school. Among the more effective strategies I had stumbled on was the fact that my new Internationally Famous mentor would be returning to his native

England in September, never to return. Summer quarter offered a rare opportunity to study with him.

To my delight, once classes resumed, Mr. Internationally Famous began once again offering me extra attention. This gave me added credibility with my classmates and made me feel so special that I began to dress a little flashier and carry myself with a little of the swagger of an up-and-coming force in the art world. That's why, when Mr. International asked me to go out with him on Saturday night, I was shocked. I honestly didn't know what to make of it. I also didn't feel like I had a choice of responses. But I relaxed knowing it couldn't be a date. Not a "date" date. He was *really old.* He said he was like forty-six. And I was just turning nineteen, so his interest couldn't be male/female. It had to be more along the lines of a genius encouraging a prodigy. I had been tapped for greatness.

Joining us that evening, as it turned out, was another summer quarter painting professor who was also mentoring a budding young female genius tapped for greatness. We drove in to San Francisco to a small club to see Charles Pierce, an internationally famous female impersonator. International fame was everywhere that night. Charles Pierce performed a large repertoire of lip-synching routines dressed as actresses from the thirties and forties. When he did Bette Davis doing Scarlett O'Hara on a swing covered in plastic flowers, the mostly gay male audience went wild. I was not sure why a man in wigs, lip-synching to records, was supposed to be so awe inspiring, but if I was puzzled by the show, I was even more puzzled when Mr. Internationally Famous put his tongue in my ear. I remember thinking, What in the world is he doing? and then, Uh-oh.

At the end of the evening, when he pulled his car up to the curb in front of my storefront, I said, "Thank you so much. Would you like to come in for some tea?" This was what I always said to friends dropping me off. "Are you sure it's okay?" was the professor's response. The way he'd said it made me wonder what it was I might be implying when I answered, "Sure."

He came inside and sat down on my ratty thrift-store sofa, the only piece of furniture I owned. The rest of the room was filled with worktables made of doors and boards suspended on sawhorses. Everywhere were piles of sawdust, left out as proof of my serious artistic intentions. I didn't just own power tools, I also knew how to use them.

"Come sit next to me," he said, patting the couch as I approached with cups of tea. I was planning to show him my shoebox full of awful but funny postcards. When I sat down beside him, he immediately put his arm around me. I was planning to show him a pile of cards that all featured a giant trout filling up the bed of a pickup truck when Mr. International leaned in to kiss me. I tried to hide my reaction. To me, kissing an old dude like the Internationally Famous Professor was like making out with Santa.

Maybe I looked to the Man of International Fame like a girl who had been around. Maybe my short skirts and my tall boots and my foul mouth had fooled him. He probably would have been surprised to learn that just a day or two earlier I had asked my best friend, "What does it mean when a guy says, 'Did you come?' " "Come where?" I asked her, "Come to what?" "I'm not sure," she replied, "I think it might have something to do with having an orgasm." "*Come* means an orgasm?" I said. "Since when did *come* mean *orgasm*?" And then I asked her, "How can you tell if you're having one?"

Next thing I knew, the Internationally Famous Professor and I were on my Murphy bed having sex. Not because I wanted to but because I didn't know how to say no to a Man of International Fame. I tried to say something. I opened my mouth to form words, but nothing came out. And, as I would also expect from a sexual encounter with Santa, I left my body during the act. I was preoccupied with unanswered questions. It was only the second time I had ever had sex, and, based on the evidence so far, I wondered what there was to like about it.

The first time had been a couple of weeks before, when I had spent the night with a psychotic art student on PCP. Earlier in the evening he had thrown his stereo out the window. I guess that was his idea of foreplay. On the bright side, he made love like a programmed animatronic robot. I knew he had no feelings for me, but that was okay. At least I wouldn't get emotionally involved. By the time it was over I felt I knew less about sex than I had when I was a virgin. Now I wondered what about it had hypnotized civilization all these centuries. How had it managed to capture the imaginations and the souls of musicians, painters, poets, and newlyweds? I had assumed that something about it would be great. Now I had absolutely no idea what.

The third time I had sex was when I was raped by the guy who broke in to my apartment the night after I had sex with the Internationally Famous Professor. I was asleep in my Murphy bed, in the farthest of the three rooms that stretched out in a row from the front door.

I heard a noise that woke me up. I thought it was the wind.

Maybe a window wasn't closed properly. When I got up to close it, I saw a guy in a dark hooded sweatshirt. For a minute it didn't compute. What didn't I understand about this? Before I had an answer, he came up behind me and put his hand over my mouth. Then he grabbed me around the neck. A wild electrical bolt went through my brain, a blinding flash of white light. Oh My God. This can't be happening, I was thinking, Who is he? What is he doing here? And then my very next thought, swear to God, was, Jesus Christ. I bet he's here to steal my power tools.

Turned out the guy must have had his own electric sander and band saw, because the power tools remained untouched. He dragged me to my bedroom and threw me down on the bed. My brain was racing, looking for a strategy, a plan of action. I had been taking abnormal psychology classes. I had read that rape was not about sex but about power, and domination. If subduing a struggling woman was arousing, I would buy myself some time by pretending to have passed out. When he moved one of my arms or legs, I let it fall limp, like a corpse. My tongue hung out of my mouth. My eyes remained closed, and I made sure they never opened. At one point he was lying on top of me, removing my clothes. And then, only a minute or so after the sex act had begun, amazingly enough, he got up off me and left the room. I wondered if maybe he'd gone to get some water to throw on me to try to wake me up. Or had he come to his senses and gone for the power tools? I didn't wait to find out. I jumped up and closed the door, then locked it and began to scream. After that I picked up the phone and called 911 and the police.

By the time they arrived, I was locked in my room alone,

sobbing, dressed in the only clothes that were handy—a short striped minidress and a pair of high leather boots. No one really spoke to me except to find out what they needed for the police report. They dusted the walls for fingerprints in silence, then sent me off in an ambulance to the county hospital. During the ride, as we sped through the streets in the middle of the night, the siren screaming, I felt embarrassed that I hadn't sustained worse injuries to justify the need for an ambulance. I wasn't hurt physically. But my mother had been right. Being emotionally involved was definitely awful.

Next thing I knew I was walking into the County General emergency room. When I saw my reflection in the glass door as I entered, I barely recognized myself. My makeup was smeared, like I'd been trick-or-treating. My hair was scraggly and sticking out. I had boarded the ambulance in such shock and haste that I hadn't thought to do any post-rape grooming.

Taking a seat by the wall in the waiting room, I didn't have the attention span for *Redbook* or *Mademoiselle*. It had all just begun to sink in, and I felt really sad and alone. I stared across the room at a black mom and her wired eight-year-old son. I didn't know why they were there, but in a couple of minutes the little boy was hanging around me, bored, wanting to talk, intruding in the way that only goofy grade-school kids can. He looked at me, as I sat miserable and silent. "Lady," he said, cocking his head and squinting as he looked at me, "If you ain't Medusa, you is Medusa's sister."

I was surprised to hear myself laugh. Not only was it funny but it was also true. I was also stunned that a kid his age had referenced Medusa. Whenever I thought of his remark, it made me laugh again. That the kid had made me laugh made it all somehow bearable. In my new roll as Medusa's Sister I was much better equipped to put things into some kind of workable perspective.

A short while later, the hospital released me. Someone needed to drive me home. My family was gone on vacation. My art school friends had gone home for the summer. So there I was with no one to call except the Internationally Famous Professor. I phoned his apartment, where I found him in the midst of mentoring another young art student genius. He was shocked to hear of my situation, though not happy to be interrupted. Still, to his credit, both he and his date showed up to give me a ride.

But a man of his International Fame had a busy schedule. And so he left after dropping me off at the scene of the crime. Now I faced an evening of staring at walls full of dusted fingerprints, wondering if the guy who had broken in was nearby, watching.

I was standing out in front of the place, afraid to go in the front door, when I met my neighbors for the first time. They were standing in the next doorway, peering out at me.

"Are you okay? What happened?" asked a slim blond man, coming over to talk. Now I could see that he and his friend were both in drag.

"Well, I guess I'm okay. Except I was raped," I said.

"Oh my God!" he said. "I am so shocked. You always hear about things like this, but you never think they will happen to anyone you know. Did he steal anything?"

"No," I said, opening the door and looking inside to see my power tools still on my worktable. Then I noticed something else. "Oh shit, he got my purse."

"Maybe he had a belt and shoes to match," said the blond guy. "Honey, why don't you come in and sit down and have a cup of tea?" I eagerly accepted rather than be alone. "I have to apologize. Kevin and I just split the last Quaalude," said blondy, "but we also have Valium, Vicodin, and speed." He held out a tin full of pills, as though he were offering me some breath mints.

"Tea will be just fine," I said.

"You're sure?" he said. "If you change your mind, just let me know. Are you a student or what?" he asked, showing me into their art deco–laden apartment.

"I'm an art student," I said.

"How fabulous!" he said. "We both do some art. Would you like to see some pictures of our show?"

"Yes," I said, happy to have a distraction. And so, as we sipped our tea, I *ooh*ed and *aah*ed over photos of them both on stage, doing assorted striptease moves in dozens of different ensembles. "This is me as Judy. Here I am as Barbra. That's Kevin as Carol Channing and Lady Bird Johnson!" he sang. "Doesn't he look fantastic? Kevin's kind of an artist in his own right."

"I've been doing some drawing," Kevin confessed, bringing out a giant sketch pad. "Do you mind if I show you my work and have you critique it?"

"No, no, not at all," I said with a lot more enthusiasm than I was feeling. So I sat still as Kevin began to turn the pages, revealing sketch after sketch of misshapen, poorly drawn, male nudes.

"Well, here you've made the arms too short," I pointed out. "They should come down below the hips. See how in most of these you have made the arms end above the waist?"

"Oh! Yes! You're right!" he said, seeing the problem. We continued discussing his technique for over an hour, during which neither one of us ever bothered to mention that all of the sketches were of men having anal sex.

Soon it was sunrise. Feeling more confident by the light of day, I returned to my apartment, packed up all my stuff, and loaded it into my car.

The whole world was different now. When I walked down the street it seemed like everyone was staring at me through a fish-eye lens. Overnight I had gotten the lead in a Fellini film. It was the end of my brand-new sense of sexual confidence. All that swagger I had just begun to brandish went right down the dumper that day. I took all my miniskirts and gave them to the Goodwill. Dressing any way but drab now seemed like a bad idea. No more accidentally dressing like a hooker without even knowing how a hooker dressed.

I stayed with someone in my class until the summer quarter ended, then I loaded up my stuff again and drove home. Of course, my parents wanted to know all about how it had gone with the Internationally Famous Professor. I made up a story about how inspiring it had all been. And then they asked to see my work. I kind of hemmed and hawed, and then I showed them the only painting I had finished. It was a self-portrait: a painting of my face with snakes coming out of my head instead of hair. Underneath I had written the words *Medusa's Sister.*

My parents looked at it. Neither one said anything. "That's it?" said my father, shrugging, baffled. My mother shook her head at him in disbelief. "For this you had to go to summer school?" she sighed.

do you take this woman?

~ em and lo

Do you take this woman to be your best friend; will you hold her hair back when she throws up, and talk trash about her ex-boyfriends; do you promise to honor and support her in good times and bad, in sickness and in health, even when she's a bitch and not getting laid, for as long as you both shall live?

Lo: Volumes have been written on love—so many attempts to define that indefinable spark, that mysterious pull that brings certain people's hearts and genitals together. It is at the center of every other Shakespeare play and Hollywood blockbuster. You could probably wrap all the sonnets ever written on the subject around the world a few times. But the topic of best friendship? Poetry on it—okay, *decent* poetry—would probably make it once, maybe twice, around a Damon-Affleck hug. For the most part, friendship is relegated to Hallmark cards and coffee table books featuring black-and-white pictures of little girls in big Easter bonnets. Best friendship gets no respect.

But isn't long-lasting friendship as compelling as romantic love? It might not be as dirty, but it takes just as much work. Even more so simply *because* there's (usually) no sex to take the edge off your partner's flaws, their annoying habit of leaving toenails on the floor or their penchant for Top 40 music. Without the biological impulse to procreate (or at least to get buck naked together), what makes two people stick it out side by side for years, if not a lifetime? Fate? Chemistry? Mutual respect? Shallow, loathsome, chartreuse-colored envy? A common interest in quail egg collecting? Same shoe size? Fear of dying alone once the divorce is final and you're estranged from your kids? Like true love, it's near impossible to elucidate. In the case of me and Em, if I were to hazard a guess, I would say it was above all a case of opposites attracting—complementing each other like two puzzle pieces, like chocolate and peanut butter, like James Carville and Mary Matlin.

It's not like I fell for Em at first sight. In fact, I was quite wary of her. While I was on vacation, she was hired by the small smart sex magazine I was working for at the time. We would be working fourteen-hour days (including weekends) together, literally inches apart. I fretted she'd be a competitive guys' girl with half a brain who'd try to manage me while she rearranged my files. I worried she'd have halitosis. Of course, it was much worse than that. Em turned out to be a sweet, charming, brilliant, and egalitarian colleague with a degree from Princeton, an endearing British accent, and a heart of gold. You know, totally annoying—if only because her presence made me painfully aware of my own shortcomings. The only thing I could complain about was her occasional tea breath.

We felt each other out and felt each other up on the dance floors of New York City, as new acquaintances who are twenty-five and drunk are wont to do. I figured maybe some of her good qualities would rub off on me, that I wouldn't simply suffer by comparison. For some reason, she never gave me any excuses about being busy and having to wash her hair. Soon, we were opting to hang out on almost all our days off, sharing the intimate details of our own sex lives after a work week of talking about other people's sex lives.

That was five years ago. Today, we still work side by side, we still write about sex, and we still dish to each other about our own sex lives every chance we get. Maybe it's because we're still learning things from and about each other. Em can finish the *Times* crossword, and I can program my Tivo with some success. She can spell *licentious* (I had to ask her how). Em would rather eat worms than emote in front of people, so I have to pull her onstage with me at karaoke bars for heart-rending and ear-shattering renditions of "Hopelessly Devoted to You." In high school, she was an acne-ridden Jesus freak who ate her lunch in the bathroom and didn't kiss a boy until college. While I wasn't Miss Popularity, I did perform in the school plays, was elected Student Council President, regrettably cheered for the football team, and had a healthy, rigorous sex life during those formative John Hughes years. Em's got a functional family in England, proving that the family that drinks together, stays together. Mine split up back in the eighties, mostly because my dad drank alone. Em keeps her emotional cards close to her chest; I let it all hang out (though Em's the one whose boobs occasionally pop out of her low-cut shirts).

If we were charged particles, I'd be the negative one, Em the positive. She's a Locke girl, I'm more Hobbesian by nature. And yes, she's a little bit country (God help me); I'm a little bit rock and roll. While she'll never say a bad word about anyone, even when she wants to (even when she *should*), I find the worst in everyone, especially when I shouldn't. Em used to assume automatic unspoken exclusivity with anyone she started seeing; after several years of dating in this city and a few slaps from me, à la Cher in *Moonstruck,* she's awake and smelling the coffee. And I've learned to send any irate business emails to Em first so she can run them through her diplomacy machine. She maintains a strong, stoic silence in the face of tragedies like 9/11, but the teenie-bopper flick *What a Girl Wants* reduces her to a quivering mass of tears. Meanwhile, I get riled up at all the cleaning product commercials featuring women doing the chores. I've dragged Em kicking and screaming into feminist consciousness and conscientiousness, and she's slowly but surely come to the dark side. Still, Em thinks dinner conversation should not include pointless political discussions on the state of the world, especially if you're not going to get up off your ass and do something about it. Unfortunately, my sofa is really comfortable. At least I'm a vegan; Em eats tortured baby cows.

She once signed a birthday card to me, "You make me want to be a better person." Cheesy movie reference aside, it was the highest compliment she could have paid me. When I play back that moment in my mind, it's in slo-mo: The party guests around us continue laughing boisterously, drinking and eating, totally unaware as our eyes lock and we have a moment of deep understanding. For she knows in that instant that I feel the same way about her, despite all our disagreements, our different approaches to life, even our conflicting views and values. We smile at each other like we're in love, the inspirational pop music swells, the camera pulls back, and the credits roll.

In Sickness . . .

Em: When it seems like you'll never be fit for anything except sobbing in an empty bathtub (because actually filling it would require undressing); when work, personal hygiene, and world hunger are inconveniences too trivial to address; when conversation is an impossible burden but solitude unbearable; when the only person you wish to seek comfort in is the one who just broke your heart—well, if you don't have someone you can bear to grieve near at times like these, you're better off never dating at all.

And so it begins each time, with a seven-dollar bottle of red wine, a stack of take-out menus, and a rental copy of *Shirley Valentine*. It's friendship CPR—an urban survival kit to nurse one of us through the first forty-eight hours of a breakup. (And it's a highly refined process, too—in an early incarnation, when it was my heart that had been broken, we attempted to add a joint to the mix. I choked and scorched my throat and remained weepy and straight, leaving Lo with remorseful giggles and me with the horrifying notion that I was too sad even to get stoned.) Mostly, over the past five years, it's been Lo's heart breaking. One man, one frequently interrupted relationship, and one best friend. We pull out the sleeper sofa, get into sweats, and get hazy together on merlot while I monitor Lo's vital signs and screen her calls.

Those first few days are the easy part, at least for me. The words of condolence can be sparse and generic, because what the hell difference do they make anyway? My sole purpose is to man the TV remote. There's no looking back in regret or anger, and no looking forward in fear, there's simply staring straight ahead at a fourteen-inch screen.

Eventually Lo is forced to admit that, despite a distinct lack of effort on her part, she's still breathing, sweating, shitting. She feels hungry for the first time since the breakup. And she owes twenty dollars in late fees at the local video store. This all translates to tasks that must be accomplished, albeit numbly. On my to-do list, meanwhile, is the Ex. He began as her friend (though much crushed upon) and then became mine too; then he was her hook-up and my friend; then her boyfriend, the fourth on our double dates, and my friend. And then? His transgressions over the years have been both horrible and clichéd, but I have committed the same and forgiven friends for worse. And yet one friendship must trump another. The Boyfriend and I have learned how to put our relationship on hold because it's easier for me not to know who he is—and who he does—in the in between. He and I follow the rules neither of romantic nor of friendly attachments. We are at once unavoidably attached and yet detached, because our relationship is in the wake of theirs.

Once Lo has forgiven him, he is, for a brief period, sheepish around me, but the discomfort never lasts. It has been a year now since I have had to forgive him for anything, and the copy of *Shirley Valentine* that I finally invested in has been gathering dust. Fortunately Lo's pull-out couch seats three.

Honor

Lo: But what if you're *not* friends with your best friend's boyfriend?

Em and I both started out as buddies with . . . let's call him X. He was cool, smart, fun—nothing not to like. We all got along swimmingly.

And then one day he touched Em's special place.

Next thing you know, he's falling in love (how could he not?) and she's going along for the ride because, really, it had been a while since she'd gotten out. Now she's got someone to cook dinner for her, someone to finish the crossword with, someone to say "I love you" to, someone to fuck. But most important, she's got someone to pick her bacne.

So what could be wrong with that? Sure, it *sounds* like a sweet deal. And it was for a while. But the deeper X fell, the more his traditional family values sprouted up like weeds in the relationship—at least my relationship with him. Now, Em is no hippie polygamist; she will be married in a church to one man for all eternity while wearing a white veil and dress. But she has had sex before (despite her slow start) and she does write about it. Apparently, writing about sex was okay for X's friends, but not for his girlfriend. His baseball-cap–wearing colleagues would check out Em's work online and then give him a good ribbing about it. That bothered him. He wouldn't attend lectures we gave because he couldn't stand to see her talking about such private matters to an audience full of men, some of whom surely possessed a mind as dirty as his. X saw the good Christian girl in her and wanted to preserve it (sans the virginity clause); after all, that upbringing is the source of her sweetness. The more he cared about her, the more he cared about what she said and did. He became possessive and judgmental.

But that role in her life was already filled—by me. Not only am I Em's friend, business partner, sister, and husband but I'm also her dad with the shotgun, and nobody's good enough for my baby. If it were up to me, I'd say who, I'd say where, and I'd say when. Em and I have lots to do before she settles down. Anyone standing in the way of that is just not going to do.

So X and I saw each other as obstacles to Em's full potential, to her becoming her true self. Needless to say, my relationship with him was strained, though we pretended it wasn't. We'd all go out to dinner and then spend entire courses in awkward silence. He couldn't properly celebrate or congratulate big steps in our careers, because that would imply approval. It didn't help that he was a brainiac who made board games—the staple of the double date—miserable for the rest of us (okay, me). Pretty soon we stopped even trying to hang out together. Which meant less time for me with Em. Which meant more resentment on my part.

Of course, it never mattered what I thought of him, or whether we got along. When it comes to romantic love, all that matters is the happiness two people share when they're alone in the privacy of their bedroom, when they open themselves up, expose their vulnerabilities and show each other their assholes. Outsiders—even best friends—may not understand it. Whether or not she was really happy, Em never let on. She never complained to me—not even about the normal, expected things that get on every significant other's nerves—probably because she was afraid that I'd use it as an excuse to put in my vote for eviction. And I never put in that vote, because I knew it ultimately wasn't mine to give.

Em and X have long broken up (I like him much better now), and I can safely say they were never right for each other. I *always* knew this, because despite his pleas, Em would never acquiesce and pick his hard-to-reach spots. She'll tell you it was a matter of principle, that popping another person's zits is "gross." But I know better and I know Em. If she had *truly* been in love, she would have squeezed away with happy abandon. Lucky is the man upon whose back Emma lays her hands. Even luckier if he gets along with me.

Communication

Em: Entire industries have been built on the tired old notion that while men would rather undergo a colonoscopy than Talk About the Relationship, women crave communication like chocolate, Manolos, or there-when-you-need-them orgasms. Yet you only have to look to our relationships with each other to see that emotional sharing is not necessarily a chick thing (and you can hold the Manolos, while you're at it). The four little words "We have to talk" strike fear in the heart of many a damsel too—and in particular in the heart of me, when they are uttered by Lo.

The Talk is not necessarily a romantic thing, it's simply an indication that you spend too much time together to let some things go unsaid. With more casual friends and acquaintances, there's room for a little dysfunction (or, as it's more commonly known, "Can't we all just get along?"). With family members, the blood ties mean that the relationship itself is the default, and even a lack of decent adult communication can't change that—so fights can often pass into history without an official resolution phase. In romantic relationships, the need for state-of-the-relationship talks is a given, even if one party has to be coerced into such talks (by their partner, by booze, by the promise of great oral, by a therapist). With a best friend, there is neither blood nor booty. And yet the relationship will at times be fraught with all the niggling emotions—jealousy, irritation, anger, insecurity, et al—familiar to more formal bonds.

People often ask us (as they no doubt wonder about married couples who work together), "How do you have anything left to say to each other?" But it's the wrong question. The one we've found ourselves asking is, When you talk seven times a day, how do you know when it's time to *really* talk? It is Lo, always, who initiates, usually on the half-year. I am like that clichéd (and slightly mythical) male who must be coerced. If I had my way, our relationship would run as smoothly as a fairy-tale (or Hollywood) romance; we'd never need to indulge in "us talk" because it would all go without saying. I get bad flashbacks to one of my most intense best friends of old—she was ten, I was nine—who cornered me during a game of hide-and-seek to say "I love you." I begrudgingly muttered it back. I meant it, of course, but couldn't understand why we had to be so weird and say it out loud. Thus, Lo wisely waits until we have drained our first glass of wine (or sangria, if it's a summer Talk) before dropping those four little words. The first few sentences are blind-date stilted, and I make less eye contact than an ADD victim with a lazy eye. But as the words begin to spill forth (in direct proportion to the sangria), no cliché is safe from us: "I feel like we've drifted apart" leads to "But you don't let me in"; "I think you'd be happier if you did this" is countered with "But that would be changing who I am"; "You lied to me" is justified as "I was afraid you'd judge me"; "You slurp your tea," is met with "Yeah, well, you don't bring me flowers anymore." Hours later, we are teary, exhausted, tipsy, and pretty damn pleased with ourselves.

Like a good colon cleansing, the Relationship Talk is a process best not anticipated or recalled in all its gory detail, lest you never dare go there again. And like enema evangelists, we're ardent proponents of the Talk for every platonic couple, and somewhat suspicious of best friends who claim not to need it (repression will bite you in the ass, people). "We should do this more often," we always say in closing, both knowing that what we really mean is, another six months will do just fine.

Fidelity

Lo: When I moved from Boston—one of the most homogeneous, anally retentive, sexually closed-minded cities in America—to New York six years ago, I figured I was going to get laid all the time. I was going to work for a *sex* magazine, after all, at the center of the internet content boom, in New York Fucking (literally) City: There were art openings and glam parties and dance fests every night of the week, and no economic downturn or Red Alert to dull the libido. Turns out I didn't get laid once that first year. Yet, when Em showed up in the middle of my dry spell, I was still the sexual adventurer, relatively speaking. She had lost her virginity a scant three years earlier, with a total body count of four; mine was up to twenty-five. I had perfected my blow-job technique over the past decade, whereas she had yet to give one. She was shocked, though flattered, when I complained she had perfect boobs—no one had ever mentioned them to her before. Em went to church; I went to the movies. She still wore sweatshirts and floral print sundresses. 'Nuff said.

But within just a few months, our job, this town, and several young men had gotten into her blood, whether through osmosis or the occasional orifice. Having spent the previous three years in a one-bar town, Em was more than happy to join me at every open-bar party in town (since unfortunately the so-called boom impacted our libidos more than our bank accounts). We'd go out, convinced we were cooler than we actually were—the only way to live in such an image-conscious city. One night we walked into a club and Em said to me without a hint of irony, "Let's scope the joint." Making out in front of boys we liked became our patented party trick. We even propositioned my future boyfriend to help us act out a porno version of a *Three's Company* episode. (Thank goodness he had a severe lack in judgment and said no, or else Em and I might not be friends today.)

But the next thing I know, she's going ahead and having her first threeway anyway—without me. Not that I necessarily would have come along for the ride if I had been invited, but just knowing I was welcome would have been nice. Soon, Em started putting notches on her belt, in her lipstick case, and up her butt—notches I had either dreamed about or gasped at. While I committed myself to one man, more or less (and off and on), Em sampled a wide variety of cocktail wieners. She discovered she could separate sex from love. She went from zero to sixties' style orgies in the blink of an eye, while I sat on the sidelines. Who was the prude now?

Best friendship can exert its own weird kind of peer pressure, a need to belong, to keep up. Deciding not to keep up can be unsettling; it can create an awkward space between you—whether it's about giving up dairy or taste-testing pussy. Like a good husband who's committed to making things work, I've tried to temper my jealousy over the years. And I've learned Em's had to temper hers too; though I refuse to believe she covets my C-cups, I know Em would give up her casual escapades for a decent boyfriend. And she still comes to me for blow-job counsel.

But for every sexual handstand of hers I've applauded, there's been one I secretly boo. I'm plagued not only by jealousy but by that other evil J word too: judgment. I don't believe much in horoscopes (even though we have a gig writing them each week), but if anything were to make me a believer, it would be that Emma lives up to her sign: the dual-natured Gemini. She may have most people fooled with her good girl image, but like I've said, Em's got a bad girl in her. In our column, the good girl dishes out advice based on a solid moral belief system; the bad girl doesn't follow that advice. The good girl believes in the sanctity of marriage; the bad girl will have sex with someone who's spoken for. The good girl knows intellectually that anyone can get an STD; the bad girl will do it without a condom.

Of course, having a dark side isn't a crime, it's human. But if people—or at least my closest friends, the people I admire most in this world—don't play by the rules, the system breaks down. Kant said so. And then what hope is there for this cold, cruel world? Besides, why should Em get to have all the fun? Like a lover who's cheated, she'll be vague, leave out important details, or flat-out lie about her indiscretions because she knows she'll have to suffer my wrath otherwise. But just like her old boyfriend, I judge because I care. I don't want her womb to become, because of some stupid—though orgasmic—one-night stand, an inhospitable place for the future babies she wants to have. And I want her to set a good godmotherly example for the kids I might have someday. She can be bad, just in a good way.

Til Death Do Us Part

Em: Of late, strangers have been asking if we're related. Sure, some of them are simply not that imaginative (we both have long brown hair), and some of them probably mean, And do you dress up in short frilly nighties when you write together? But the question has come often enough that we've been forced to admit it: Like retirees in matching track suits, we have begun to blend. We've taken on each other's mannerisms and fashion sense (even if Lo sometimes calls it "copying"); we finish each other's sentences (even if Lo sometimes calls it "interrupting"); we accidentally order for each other in restaurants (even if Lo sometimes calls it "creepy"). And we say "we" an awful lot.

We seem more married than some of our married friends. Regrettably, for as long as conservatism rules, it won't earn me a green card. But it *has* given us an answer to another question we're frequently posed: What makes you relationship experts if you've never been married? (Were the inquirers privy to our late-night chatter, they might add, ". . . and if Em's still incapable of falling for a guy who loves her?") The pat answer is that those who can't do, teach. And it's not a bad one, either—what do you care if your personal trainer is a little saggy around the edges if they can whip *your* butt into shape?

But the unabridged reply is that our friendship is the best laboratory we know. Though New York is one of the least hostile environments for an unmarried woman in her thirties (have you visited the South lately?), it is nevertheless not particularly pleasant to navigate alone. But if a potential spousal candidate has yet to present himself (or—gasp!—we choose to go without), we can construct a husband from a friend. As we grow older, we grow more particular about what we want from both lovers and friends; the tendency is to expect more from the former and less from the latter. But by learning to expect more from each other as friends, Lo and I have learned how to demand both more and less from a partner. What I once regarded as "pushy" I can now see as communicative; what Lo once regarded as "pushover" behavior she can appreciate as open-minded.

"Best friend" is one of those terms people are often embarrassed to use once they hit their thirties (or even their twenties or their teens). It brings to mind playground bickering, pinkie promises, and the underlying threat that your best friend might one day trade you in for a more popular model. And best friendship is exacting too—many a marriage has crumbled under the strain a couple can feel at being all things to each other. It's no wonder we shy away from such expectations in friendship. But tell me this: How many of your casual friends or acquaintances would be moved by a sense of responsibility to hand you a pair of cosmetic scissors and say, "You've got a rather prominent nose hair you should take care of"? And would she then quickly add, "I just trimmed a few of my own," so you didn't feel as alone in this world as Sasquatch?

penelope

എ erika krouse

A new woman's name had been creeping into their conversation. Whenever Allison asked Ford about his day,
he'd say, "Oh, you know, nothing special. I hung out with Hester." Or: "That's funny you said that. Hester said the same
thing. So . . . bizarre." Hester was a bullish college dropout
with splotchy skin. She worked as a cashier at a sushi place,
handing off money and fish. She always looked like she just
rolled out of a sloppy bed, with creases on her cheeks. She resembled the insecure narrator in teen romance novels, the
one who grows on you and, in the end, somehow manages to
get the cute guy. In that world, she's the one you root for.

But Allison and I don't live in that world. This Hester was

a Brazilian jiujitsu wrestler and a downhill mountain bike racer. She had no fear. She had no mercy. She had no female friends. She had just broken up with Ford's best friend, and now she and Ford spent every evening in the unair-conditioned jiujitsu studio, sweating on rubber mats together and pretending to break each other's arms. She was ugly and determined. Allison was terrified. I was Allison's friend. Still am, in fact, but then it was a budding best-friendship, at a time of stasis for both of us. I was utterly single, and she was utterly coupled. I was dating men for the free meals, and Ford was making Allison buy her own birthday cake. Neither of us was satisfied with much, besides each other. Remember when you were little, and you found a friend who was exactly your size and weight, so you climbed on the seesaw together? And just hung there? The seesaw stayed exactly parallel with the ground, and you just dangled in midair, grinning, while everyone around you on the playground threw rocks at each other and screamed and won and lost? That's what being friends with Allison was like.

I hadn't officially met Ford. I had seen him several times, I think. In fact, I had tried Brazilian jiujitsu myself, and he must have been there at the time, but I couldn't recognize him out of a group of, say, three. He shaved his head to hide his receding hairline and always wore a gray sweatshirt. Allison usually dressed like a male transvestite—rhinestones, fake fur. So they didn't really match, although they had been together for eight years. They had met when they were nineteen. They had survived cheating (Ford's), an aborted pregnancy (Allison's), and the fact that in eight years, Ford had never asked Allison to get married or move in with him. He never gave her a flower. He never gave her a birthday card. At one point in their relationship, Allison disappeared to Antarctica, to make a fresh start. She spent six months at McMurdo Research Station, the frigid end of the earth, surrounded by white ice. The buildings were on stilts, and the plumbing had been leaking and freezing for over fifteen years. Between research assignments, Allison lay on her stomach underneath the building, thinking about Ford and chipping fifteen years' worth of rock-hard frozen urine from under the bathroom with a pneumatic drill.

So they survived piss-ice. They survived Ford's eating habits. He ate the same thing every day. For breakfast it was eggs and tortillas. At ten o'clock he ate an apple with peanut butter on it. For lunch, a bean and buffalo meat burrito, and so on. They survived his narcissism. When they went on vacations, they had to plan their activities around his gym workouts.

But surviving is not living. And Ford didn't want to be survived. He wanted, well, probably to be left alone. Hester could do that for him. Allison couldn't, because she loved him, like an old scab on her heart that she had to pick at and touch tenderly to see if it still hurt.

Allison called me and said, "Well, Ford hasn't returned my calls in two weeks. I think that constitutes a message."

"But I thought he asked you to move in," I said.

"No. The last thing he said was that he was going to think about maybe what it would be like if we moved in together."

"But you sleep there, you practically *do* live there. When you're getting along."

"Anyway." She was trying to hold herself together, but her voice shook. "I'm moving my shit out next week. Maybe that'll wake him up."

Allison called to give him fair warning. She didn't really want to do this thing. But he never called her back, so we went to Ford's house while he was at his jiujitsu class. It was a dark spring night, right before the days got longer.

Me, I was lucky. I hadn't been in love in years. There had been a few near misses, but mostly I had stopped taking it all seriously. My dating philosophy had an acronym: NJO. Not Just One. I kept a list of men and changed their rankings every week. Some of these men were imaginary. Most dates, I just hoped we'd get to have sex before the guy pissed me off. I had a standard exit line, one I spat out when all was lost, right before I said my last good-bye. It went like this: "Listen, [name], there are three billion men on this planet. I can get any one of *them* to treat me like shit. It doesn't have to be you."

But Allison was in love with Ford. Not out of desperation, either. She could have had any of the other three billion. She was, is, very beautiful. She's naturally blondish, but dyes her hair black. She has clear, blue eyes. She lifts weights, the heavy ones on long metal poles. She likes hard-core punk music. She wears clothes with Martians and cartoon characters on them. But these things are just styles, tastes. The heart of Allison, well, the heart of Allison was right here, in this place. Ford's ugly house.

It was a dump, in one of the more expensive neighborhoods. Ford's rich father had probably paid for most of it, but Allison didn't know the details. Either way, it was a half-million-dollar eyesore, despite Allison's landscaping and decorating. The paint was brown, and the front porch was missing steps. There were gaping holes outside. And inside, there was a shallow indentation in the wall where Ford had tried to kick in the drywall. It was a new dent. Allison pointed to it as she walked in. "I bet that was over me," she said. She left Ford's dogs in their crates, grunting and snuffling.

We had barely inhaled the dog-breath air before Allison's head snapped around. With two fingers, she slowly pulled a ratty orange jacket off the coatrack. It was in a woman's size. "This isn't my jacket," Allison said. She looked at me, then walked into the bedroom. She pointed to Ford's bed. "Those aren't his sheets," she said. The sheets were blue.

"Maybe he bought new ones," I said.

But Allison was already in the bathroom. There was a rummaging sound, then silence. I walked over.

She was staring inside the medicine cabinet. "That's *her* toothbrush," Allison said. "Next to *my* diaphragm."

"Whose toothbrush?"

She looked at me slowly. "Hester's," she said.

It did look like a hussie-toothbrush, brand-new and carefully rinsed, not presumptuous enough to sit in the stand next to Ford's, which was upright and alone. No, it wasn't alone. Allison's was still in there, because she pulled it out of its hole and tapped her chest with it. "Mine," she said. Then she was in the bedroom, raking through some drawers. Man, she had a lot of clothes here. Half of the closet, and two full drawers.

Allison pulled out a T-shirt and a pair of women's underwear. She threw them on the floor with a growl.

"*These* aren't mine," she said, now running for the telephone.

I considered telling her to wait until she calmed down. But when would that be? The underwear lay on the floor, inert. It had balloons on it. It had holes in it. Allison called the jiujitsu studio and asked for Ford. I didn't even pretend not to listen. She started out strong: "I want to know how long you've been fucking her. Now."

Then: "Hey. You can't do this to me again, Ford. Ford. Ford. How could you do this to me? Again?"

Then: "I *knew* you were falling in love with her. Are you in love with her? Ford, I want to—Can we—"

Then: "Eight years with you, and I deserve more respect than— Ford, I deserve—I de—"

Then: "Fuck you *fuck* you, you fucking fuck you fuck fuck fuck—"

After she hung up the phone, Allison screamed. Toe pointed straight out, she kicked the wall, right where Ford had dented it. I winced. Her foot bounced back, and she cried out sharply. Her face was a wreck. "I think I broke my toe," she said, hopping and crying. She limped into the kitchen.

I studied the wall. I'm a black belt in karate, but I had never kicked a wall, or boards, or whatever. We don't do flashy stuff like that, but I was curious. It's drywall, after all. I drew my leg back and kicked Allison's ex-boyfriend's wall. My foot sank through, puncturing a neat, foot-shaped hole in the surface. It was surprisingly easy. I was pleased with myself. I went and found Allison, who was crumpled against a wall.

"Let's trash his house," I said.

"No," she said, looking up in terror, and I could see that she was still in the shock of love, still hoping that she'd be welcome again in this place. She dug her head into her hands. "He said, 'This time, it's love.'" She cried from deep inside her chest, wild and true as an oboe, unpracticed. It was the worst sound I'd ever heard. I didn't know how to help, where to put my hands. Her hair trembled.

"We'll kill him," I said.

He said, " 'This time, you're right.' "

"Fucking asshole."

Allison shot up, ran into the closet again. Then she was back. I choked. She was holding a vibrator.

Crying, she said, "This is what he bought me for my birthday."

Before I go on, things eventually worked out for Allison. She met a man, and then another man, and then another man who is *really* great, even though he grew up Mormon. His parents wore sacred underwear, called "the Garment," which looks like a union suit and has to go under your normal underwear. Even (and especially) on your wedding day, you have to wear the Garment. But Allison's new boyfriend doesn't wear the Garment, and he drinks beer and has premarital sex and is pro-choice and votes Democrat and they love each other. But, again, Allison certainly didn't know about any of this, then. Then, she was crying her guts out as she threw things into plastic bags and wished she were dead.

It took us two hours to clear out the accumulation of eight years' worth of Allison's careful insinuation into Ford's life. There were the obvious things, of course, but there were also judgment calls—books, CDs, gifts. Even refrigerator magnets seemed vested with significance. To take one thing, but to leave another—well, that was now a statement, and these things had to be weighed and balanced out. Whenever Allison held something in her hand and squinted, I said, "Leave no trace." At which she stuck it in a bag and moved on. I pointed to the vibrator, sitting on the kitchen table. "Do you, um, want that?"

"I don't want him to use it on her," Allison said. "But I won't use it again. It's kind of pathetic to leave your cheating boyfriend's house carrying a vibrator."

"Yeah."

"Except it wasn't really for me," she said.

"What?"

Allison put a dustpan down. She seemed to be considering something.

"Spill it," I said.

"It's personal," she said. "I mean, for better or worse, it was something we shared, something we—" Allison's glance stuck on Hester's underwear, still on the floor. She bared her teeth. "Okay, fuck him. Fuck. Him. So he gives me this vibrator for my birthday, as a present. Then he asks me to use it on *him*."

I looked at her.

She put her hands on her hips. "Well, for God's sake, we were together for eight years. We had to come up with something original. Anyway." Allison's eyes were red around the rims. "The first and last time we used it, I lubed it up and switched it on and put it, you know, inside him. And it was okay, I mean, he liked it. He really liked it. But it was slippery, and hard to keep a good grip, especially with the buzzing and everything."

"I'll bet."

She frowned. "Then something weird happened."

"What?"

"Well, his . . . body started sucking the thing in, I mean *in*. I was trying to grasp it with both hands but it kept going deeper, until the handle was gone. So I said, "Oh no, Honey, oh no, *push!*" He panicked and pushed so hard, it flew out of him and catapulted across the room. Four, five feet at least."

After a few seconds of stunned silence, we howled like dogs, and his dogs started to howl, too. Allison grabbed me, gasping and pointing with a shaking finger. "It landed right over there and spun around a few times. Oh my God." We started up again and couldn't stop until Allison started crying herself. But even then, she had to stop crying to laugh, and stop laughing to cry.

It was time to leave, but Allison didn't move, so I waited. We sat slumped over, leaning against Ford's bed with the slut's sheets on it. It smelled like human dander, fresh flesh.

It had been years since I had taken a risk. I admired Allison, and felt sorry for her. And something else. Jealousy, I think. Because I wasn't capable of that kind of love, not anymore. Not since I was a teenager, really. Allison was tough enough to cling to a cliff for a man. Her love was even tougher than she was. And isn't that noble? Or not? I didn't know. Maybe she knew. Exhausted, I pressed my forehead against the mattress until I heard Allison's voice next to me.

"Nobody prepares you for this shit," she mumbled. "It's always happy endings in the movies."

"Yeah. That's what people want," I said.

"I thought that if I just hung in there."

"You did. For eight years."

"People wait longer than that. In the *Odyssey,* Odysseus's wife waited longer than that for him to come back after he was done vacationing and cheating on her with sea nymphs. She just wove that blanket and unraveled it every night. What was her name? Penelope. She waited for him. And so did their dog."

"I think the dog died."

"But this kind of thing happens, too. All the time," Allison said. "I mean, sometimes the ugly ogre eats your man. Sometimes you wait, giving everything, and he takes everything." She touched the bedspread with one finger, tracing a worn pattern. She looked up. "Sometimes you need to forget the man and just *save yourself.*"

The light from the hall shaded her pretty face. Her eyes glittered in the dark. Allison reached out for my hand.

"Please, Erika," she said. "Write that."

the feast of san gennaro

ભ્ય jennifer weiner

Years after this happened, when the Clinton-Lewinsky scandal turned oral sex into a dinner-table topic, I remembered being astonished at the people who'd insist that oral sex was indeed sex—and hence, that oral sex was cheating.

I don't know where I got the idea that it wasn't. I know it wasn't my school or my mother who taught me that nothing really counted as sex unless it involved the old standard of penis and vagina. But, like Monica, like lots of women I knew, I lived my twenties by a few guiding principles: Food eaten standing, right out of the refrigerator, had no calories; clothes bought with a credit card wouldn't actually affect my three-digit bank balance; and oral sex didn't count.

I met David for the first time a few months after I'd moved

to Philadelphia. He was a year or two younger than me; fair-haired, light-eyed, broad-shouldered, with the comfortably roomy physique of a former high school football player, even though he'd actually played the clarinet in the band. He was a struggling musician, which made him perfect for me. At that time in my life, I was dating a lot of struggling men. There'd already been two struggling writers, a struggling actor, and a struggling artist. A struggling musician felt like the natural next step.

He was a friend of a friend of a friend, a high school buddy of one of my writer pal's ex-roommates, and one Friday night we wound up at happy hour together. I sipped a margarita while he loaded his plate again and again with free appetizers from the steam table and zucchini slices with ranch dip. Broke, but cute, I thought, as we exchanged abbreviated versions of our life histories with our fingers brushing over the complimentary mozzarella sticks.

I had a car. He had a TransPass. At the end of the night, I drove him home. "Home" turned out to be forty-five minutes away from downtown, an apartment that a great-uncle, recently departed for a nursing home, had lived in, and where David, at twenty-three, was living rent-free. It was a tiny one-bedroom apartment that smelled of pipe smoke and Vicks VapoRub. Everything in it was brown—the carpet, the couches, the walls, and the ceilings (the pipe smoke, I figured). But there was a guitar leaning against the closet door, and a keyboard set up in the living room. I parked myself on the couch, giggly after three margaritas and his shoulder against mine in my little Honda, and listened as he played and sang "You Belong to Me."

A few nights after that, we had dinner, followed by more flirting, and another ride home along an unlovely stretch of I-95. And afterward, I seem to recall some kissing on Great-uncle's brown corduroy couch. You belong to me, I thought as the rough weave pressed against my bare arms and his lips slid softly against mine and his long fingers curled against the side of my neck. I imagined our future, more drinks in more bars, movies and dinners, boyfriend and girlfriend.

After that came nothing.

I did the things you do when a guy you like's not calling. I stared at the phone. I called my answering machine every hour, on the hour. I met with my girlfriends and spent hours dissecting his personality; every word he'd said, what he'd ordered for dinner, the way he'd kissed me. Maybe I'd talked too much. Maybe I'd been too eager or, alternately, not eager enough. Maybe he didn't like the way I looked. Or maybe he only liked it when he'd been drinking. That, I thought, was the worst-case scenario. We couldn't stay drunk forever. After all, we weren't in college any more.

Finally, figuring I had nothing left to lose, one night I called him at home. He stammered something uncomfortable. I had a nice time with you, but. But what? I didn't ask. I didn't want to know. The answer was only going to hurt my feelings worse than his rejection already had. I'd thrown myself at guys in college, and, as a result, I'd memorized multiple versions of the ever-popular I-like-you-as-a-friend speech. But now I'd graduated, I was out on my own; I had a fabulous apartment, fun people to hang out with, a job I wasn't struggling at. If David didn't want me, well, that was his loss.

Months went by. Years went by. I'd see his band's name occasionally in the listing sections of the city's free weeklies, playing at one club or another, and I'd think of him, feeling a little angry, a little wistful—puzzled, more than anything else—until eventually it was just another band, and he turned into just another name I'd read, another guy who didn't matter anymore. I acquired a boyfriend who lived a convenient two hours away. We saw each other on the weekends, but my weeknights, and my apartment, were my own.

When I met David for the second time I'd been on a diet. Ten pounds, fifteen, twenty, twenty-five pounds, gone forever! (Forever, in my case, meant six months, but I didn't know that then.) I walked around light-headed and giddy from the hunger, trying to subsist on the compliments, imagining that each "Wow, you look great!" was something I wanted to eat and couldn't.

And there he was again: at another bar, another happy hour, surrounded by an identical number of cronies, both of us three years older.

He wore a plaid shirt that had been washed to the point of transparency, and the points of the collar curled in toward the skin of his neck, where I could see a vein fluttering faintly, just underneath the skin.

"So how've you been?" he asked, staring at me intently.

I gave him a mysterious smile and said nothing. I'd learned a few things since the last time I'd spoken to him, since I'd called up to ask, Did I do something wrong? And being attached gave me a certain detachment. I thought of it like an experiment. If X actions yielded Y results last time, what will happen if I don't do anything at all?

He bought me a drink (vodka, straight up, as low-calorie a

drink as I knew), let his hand brush against my back, then leaned against me as the music got louder, and the bar got hotter, and the crowd pushed us closer together.

"So are you seeing anyone?" he asked. His tone was both teasing and rueful, and his breath was warm in my ear. Oh, he looked good. Better, I had to admit, than my guy in New Jersey, the one I was diligently trying to convince myself that I was actually in love with. And he smelled wonderful. . . . I leaned close to his neck. Scotch and cologne. If my guy smelled of anything, he smelled of old marijuana smoke and Downy fabric softener (each week, he'd pile his laundry into a bag and drive forty-five minutes down the turnpike to his mother, who'd wash it, fold it, and load it into his car).

"Actually, I am. Your loss," I said, tracing a finger along the lip of my glass in a deliberate and meaningful fashion.

His cheeks heated up. He looked disappointed and, in his disappointment, even cuter than before. Your loss, I thought again and took another sip of vodka. I was thinking about the bathrooms, and whether they'd be big enough for the both of us; whether I could just grab his hand and tug him after me, take him inside and go at it without even turning on the lights. My lips on his neck, his hands on my hips, bent over the sink. . . . No, I told myself sternly. Not going to happen. He was probably just teasing me, or being nice, or something, and even if he was serious, it would be cheating, and I didn't cheat.

I shook my head to clear it and headed for the door. It was warm for September, and the air outside, after the smoke and beer fumes of the bar, felt like a silk scarf over my shoulders. "Can I call you?" David asked, leaning close enough for me to feel his breath on my lips.

I rocked back on my heels, thinking it over. Yes, I had a boyfriend, but he was two hours away, and what he didn't know wouldn't hurt him, and it wasn't like I intended to make a habit out of this, and I was hungry, so hungry, hungry all the time, drooling every time I walked past Jim's Steaks at Fourth and South and smelled the meat and grilled onions—then walked to my apartment to weigh out four virtuous ounces of boneless skinless chicken breast. Didn't I deserve something on the side? Didn't I deserve a treat?

"Don't call me," I said. "I'll call you." I wrote his phone number down on the back of a business card. Three nights later, on a Friday night, I placed a dutiful twenty-minute call to New Jersey, recited my "I love you," hung up the phone, and lay on the bed for a minute with my eyes closed and visions of bending over the sink in a cramped bar bathroom dancing in my head. Then I groped for the phone with my eyes still closed and dialed David's number, which I hadn't realized I'd memorized until that moment.

"Are you home?" I asked, and then laughed—if he was picking up the phone, of course he was home. I dropped my voice to a parody of a leer. "Are you alone?"

He was. "Want me to come over?"

"Noooo," I said, drawing out the word, lying on my back on my bed, squeezed into the smallest pair of jeans I'd ever owned. Whether my breathlessness was caused by lust or a too-tight waistband, I wasn't sure. "Tell me where you live," I said. "I'll come by."

So: the booty call. The first of my so-called adult life. Thankfully, David had ditched the northeast section of town, so I didn't have to drive very far. No more tobacco-scented living room hung with pictures of World War II. He lived less than a mile away, in a tiny studio apartment James Bond would have loved. The blue-tiled bathroom was encased in bubbled glass with a porthole cut into the shower, and the bed was front and center, the only furniture in the living/dining/bedroom. It was ten o'clock at night.

He took me by the hand to show me around. I took him by the other hand and tugged him onto the bed. "Do you want something to drink?" he asked as he rolled left and I shifted right and we found each other in the center of the bed, "something to—"

"Shhh," I said. The kisses went on and on, and there were no sounds in that one room but the CD he'd set on repeat (His own band's, I thought) and the soft noises of our lips and tongues. And then he rolled on top of me, propped up on his arms. His face in the darkness was a stranger's, and I felt an instant of unease. I didn't know him, not really. I didn't know his parents' names, or where he'd gone to high school, or how old he'd been when he'd lost his virginity. Anything could happen in this room, I thought. It should have scared me, but instead it just made me more excited. I reached for his zipper. "Hold still," I told him, as he sighed and rolled onto his back.

It wasn't cheating, I told myself as I eased his boxers over his hips and took him in my hand (he was smaller than my boyfriend in New Jersey, I noted, but at least he didn't smell like Downy). Cheating would be if he took off my jeans, which wouldn't be happening, because I wasn't letting him get anywhere near the zipper, because then he'd see that I hadn't quite been able to get the button closed. True, he managed to unfasten my bra (three hooks, one-handed—I was impressed), but while he pulled it up around my neck and was groping my breasts with heady abandon, my shirt was still on, so that was okay. Not cheating, I thought as I bent down and pursed my lips, which were swollen from our kissing, then pressed them in an O against his side and directed a warm stream of air against him, holding perfectly still and breathing, breathing, breathing until he writhed and grabbed at my hair. At least I was the one pacing things, directing the action, calling the shots.

I pulled my face away and held still, blinking so he could feel my eyelashes, and nothing else, against his tender skin. Not cheating, I told myself. And nothing was going to come of it, anyhow. It wasn't like I wanted a relationship with him any more, evidently, than he'd wanted one with me. The next day I'd be back with my boyfriend in New Jersey, and he'd be doing whatever it was he did, reprising "You Belong to Me" for some lucky lady. For now, I could just lose myself in the smell of his skin, the heat of his hands, the pleasure of the pleasure I was giving him, the long, slow, delicious, sweet, drawn-out, very impressive, super-erotic—

He wrenched his hips violently, bumping my nose with his erection. "Sorry, sorry," he gasped. I wrinkled my nose, coughing, wiping my cheeks. "Here, let me get you a towel."

He produced something off-white and threadbare from the James Bond Memorial Bathroom and lay beside me. "That was so good," he said.

"Mmm," I murmured into his neck.

"Can I . . . can we . . ."

I shook my head. We kissed. The CD he'd had on repeat

since I'd walked through the door hissed to itself, then started playing again. I closed my eyes. I knew what I should be feeling. I should be wracked with guilt, shaken with shame, tormented by thoughts of my Downy-scented boyfriend sleeping the sleep of the just in his chaste bed in New Jersey, atop sheets his mother had probably ironed. But it wasn't cheating. There'd been, technically, no sex, and he hadn't done anything for me, so I was morally in the clear. I wriggled against him, sighing in contentment, thinking that, for the first time since I'd started this wretched diet, I felt surfeit, satisfied; full.

At midnight he walked me out to my car. My lips were still swollen, but my jeans were still buttoned, which, I figured, made up for my bra, which I'd eventually pulled off, wadded up, and crammed into my purse. We were holding hands, and I thought, This is the last time I'll ever hold hands with him. I'd had some variation of that thought—this is the last time I'll ever touch him, kiss him, see him—about every boyfriend I'd ever broken up with, or who'd ever broken up with me, and usually it made me feel as if I was being stabbed in the stomach. But this time, in the soft spring air, with boughs heavy with brilliant fall leaves arching above us, it only felt bittersweet.

I think he said, "Thank you." And I said, "You're welcome." I think we both knew, without saying anything, that this would be the last time we'd meet this way—the first, the last, the only. And it was fine.

The next morning I trotted off dutifully to my Weight Watchers meeting, where I discovered I'd lost four pounds. "What's your secret?" asked the sad-eyed woman at the scales. "Infidelity," I told her. Everyone laughed.

When the meeting was over, I took the train to New York City, where I'd be meeting my boyfriend for dinner. I was early and I had time to kill, so I took the subway down to Little Italy. It was the Feast of San Gennaro, and the air was full with the smell of every delicious thing I'd been denying myself for months: roasting pork, grilled sausages with sweet onions and peppers, cotton candy, soft-serve custard, fried zeppoli dusted with powdered sugar. There were barrels of olives glistening with oil, trays of ricotta cannoli, and slices of cheesecake; paper twists of fried calamari and wax-paper cups of fresh-squeezed lemonade. I walked along Mulberry Street like an ascetic, like a saint passing through lions or walking over hot coals. I didn't eat a bite.

one way to stay warm in winter

꩜ thisbe nissen

One summer after college a bizarre coincidence results in the near-simultaneous deaths of my great-uncle and the grandmother of my best friend, Lexy. Lexy and I are each left enough inheritance money that we won't have to work for a year. I can write fiction and she can paint full-time if we live on instant oatmeal and Huber Bock ($6.99 a case at the discount food mart!) and are willing to move twenty miles outside town to a decomposing old schoolhouse the owners are trying to get onto the historical register and in the meantime are renting out to wayward masochistic creative types like us. Winter heat promises to be sporadic, indoor possum encounters frequent, the likelihood of human contact unlikely, and outside distraction from the tortured intensity of art nonexistent.

The schoolhouse could house fifteen comfortably, seven and a half if everyone wanted a bedroom *and* an office. But with just one more housemate, the three of us could swing the rent by ourselves and have *tons* of space and enough money left over to go out for a hamburger every once in a while. We put an ad in the local alternative weekly, but it seems everyone has their housing figured out already. The ad is answered by one lone, tall, chiseled, evasive sculptor in expensive leather shoes. "Uh-oh," I whisper to Lexy as the sculptor inspects the rust-stained bathroom. "We're both going to like him, aren't we?" she whispers back. "We could share," I offer. "That's one way to stay warm this winter," she says.

He moves in, insults our slovenly housekeeping skills, keeps all his food in an airtight file box in the fridge, spurns my mildly drunken advances, comes out as a born-again Christian, and insists he is too poor to pay his share of the phone, electricity, water, and gas bills. "Sell your shoes," Lexy suggests. "Or just move out," I urge. Huffily, put-upon, he is gone by morning.

We are once again in desperate need of a housemate. And then one night by the pool table at a bar in town I meet a relentlessly cocky man who is just good-looking enough to get away with his conceit and just dorky enough to be endearing in spite of himself. He has the kind of sleepy, scruffy looks that knock me sideways, a way of carrying himself that makes me want him, both to have him and to break him, wake him up, make him pay attention. Perhaps this is because he doesn't appear to be interested in me in the slightest. I am not good at relationships. I have a tendency to only want to sleep with people I dislike. We chat briefly. He's a vegan playwright living in a cruddy apartment in town. He hates it. He's got a month-to-month lease; he's looking for something else. I nod, scratch, sink the eight ball, feign disinterest in everything he tells me.

The next night I bring Lexy to the bar. "He needs a place to live," I tell her, "and he's cute. And all other things in our lives being relatively stable right now . . . just meet him," I urge. "Just see what you think."

The bar door creaks as we enter, and people turn to see who's there so that they may then turn away, lavishly disappointed. Except for the man, who is there again by the pool table; when his eyes hit on Lexy they can't seem to quit her. I am accustomed to this; Lexy is, almost inarguably, the most beautiful person most people have ever seen. She is ethereally beautiful. Hers is fairy-tale beauty, magic-potion beauty, beauty that promises both daring adventures and happy endings, poison apples and white horses. She is, as far as most men appear to be concerned, as beautiful as a dream. And this man is no different from the rest. He floats toward her as though propelled by a force greater than himself. He appears unable to place me, standing awkwardly beside her. His hand shoots out to Lexy. "Hey, I'm John," he tells her, as though this is important information, selectively imparted.

"John what?" says Lexy. I want to cheer! What spunk she has, my Lexy!

"John Smith," says John Smith.

I bust out laughing.

"What?" says John Smith.

"Your folks really went out on a limb there, didn't they?"

He looks at me, vaguely pitying. I am *the friend*. The not-so-beautiful, socially strange sidekick-of-a-friend.

"Lexy," says Lexy. John Smith has not let go of her hand. He is unwilling—perhaps unable—to let go of Lexy's hand.

Vast quantities of mercilessly cheap beer are consumed. John and Lexy become lip-locked by the jukebox, which is stuck on Tom Waits, though no one seems to mind. They kiss and kiss, and make everyone else want to kiss and kiss and kiss. The air in the bar goes thick and liquid as syrup. Bodies ooze past and seem to slip through one another. It's mid-August and no one has kissed enough this summer. To even consider asking John Smith to move into the school-house is possibly the least sane thing I have thought in a long time.

"Come home with me," John is begging Lexy.

"Help," Lexy begs me. "I'm being coerced. . . ."

"She's not going home with you," I tell John. "Unless she wants to," I concede. "Do you want to?" Lexy shakes her head soupily. "She's very chaste," I explain to John.

"You don't have to have sex with me," John allows, un-flinchingly earnest, eager to please.

"Oh, well," I say, "if she doesn't *have* to. . . . Did you hear that, Lex? He says you don't *have* to have sex with him."

Lexy smiles, tries to open her eyes, cannot. "Home," she says. "Home . . ."

"Sorry," I tell John, "you heard the lady." I steady Lexy as she tries to stand.

John looks up at me from his crouch at Lexy's feet. "What's your name again?" he asks, skeptical, like he thinks I might not have one.

"Thisbe," I say, enunciating clearly.

"Oh," says John, his suspicions apparently confirmed.

We've had caller ID installed at the schoolhouse because Lexy can't live without it; she has too many exes still halfheartedly stalking her and cannot seem to be anything but genuinely nice and friendly to every schmuck who sees her across a bar and falls in love. She gets flowers from corporate business accounts, collect calls from foreign countries, letters stamped IN-MATE CORRESPONDENCE, proposals from airplane seatmates and supermarket cashiers. And now she gets phone calls from Smith, John, who has tracked her down and calls hourly for two days straight.

"What should I do?" Lexy asks.

"Do you want to see him?"

"No . . . I don't think so, not like that."

"So pick up the phone and tell him that," I advise.

"But what about asking him to move in?"

"You *don't* want to date him but you *do* want him to move in?"

Lexy is serious. "Well," she begins, "I don't feel any great burning need to date him—though he was very fun to kiss. . . ." She considers this a moment. "No. No interest in dating him. But we aren't looking at any other options housematewise and we're not going to be able to swing the rent another month alone. And I *definitely* don't want to be dating him if he moves in. That'd just be fucked up. You know? And I don't want it to be like the two of us, and you. This is *our* place. It should be him moving into *our* place." She stops herself. "Unless *you* want him?" she asks, all earnestness, like he's hers to offer. Which maybe he is.

"I don't think *that's* going to happen," I say.

"Well, not if you don't want it to," she says, "but if you do . . ."

I wish I could make myself say I have no interest at all. But Lexy knows me too well. "I don't think I'm his type," I say.

"You sneered every word you spoke to the man!"

"What's your point?" I ask sheepishly. I know her point well.

"Would that there were a middle ground between us," Lexy muses. She is right. We have spoken of this often, how *together* we'd make a great person: my disdain and her politeness, her trust combined with my suspicions. Something in between my remove from relationships and her headlong plunges into them. Together we'd be both of our ideals.

"Your call," I tell Lexy. "If it's not weird for you, after kissing him and all . . . I mean, he can't be worse than Mr. Italian Shoes?" I am trying to muster conviction but manage only guarded skepticism. He could very well, it seems clear, be far worse than Mr. Italian Shoes.

Lexy finally returns John's calls. We've formulated a plan. We will pick him up in town and bring him back to the schoolhouse for dinner. He has, as of yet, no car. If he is to move in, that will have to be remedied. We'll also probably first have to ask him if he wants to move in.

To dinner John brings a jug of very cheap Gallo Burgundy identical to the half-jug of the same we've already set on the table. We finish our jug, then start on his. I cook lentils and rice and steam some kale I find growing by the back porch. John is complimentary to a fault, but he's trying so hard that I almost can't fault him for it. He is so thrilled to be here, invited to dinner by Lexy. His gratitude seems boundless.

I excuse myself after dinner to make a phone call. John showers me with a torrent of thanks and more culinary compliments as I leave the room. It's as though he thinks flattering me is the shortest route to Lexy's bed. As I head upstairs I hear them go out to the porch for a cigarette. It seems abundantly clear that they will not have time to do so before they are so wrapped up in kissing they forget all about nicotine.

Upstairs, pretending to read the latest issue of *Communities: A Journal of Cooperative Living,* I become convinced that Lexy has abandoned the plan altogether and given herself over to the wine and to John and to the pure sensation of kissing, to which I am sure I would be similarly giving myself were I in Lexy's position. Lexy will, I convince myself further, change her mind and opt to keep John in her life as a cute boy to kiss for awhile instead of making him the third housemate. After all, she'll say, you can live with anyone, but how many people do you really want to kiss? I know there is a logical counterargument to this argument, but I can't seem to access what it might be. I fish an address book out from under my desk and comb through it once again for people to call about the rooms for rent.

Half an hour later there's a knock on my door.

"It's me," Lexy says. She checks behind her as she enters, leaving the door ajar. Her face is flushed with wine, and kissing, and excitement. "We have something to talk to you about," she giggles. "He's in the bathroom. . . ." She glances back to the door again. She narrows her eyes at me, questioning. "So," she says slowly, "what do you think?"

"I think," I say, "the question is what do *you* think, ma'am?"

"Oh no," Lexy grins delightedly, "the question is what do *you* think?"

And then John is in the doorway, determinedly steady on his feet, the Gallo jug in one hand, three cups in the other. He, too, is grinning.

"You people look frighteningly happy," I tell them.

"Well . . . ," Lexy begins. She looks to John. As if to ask if this is okay, what she's about to do. He's giving her full go-ahead. He's pouring the wine. She looks to me then, asking my permission to proceed. We're going crazy places, her eyes are telling me. "Have some more wine," she says and pushes a glass into my hand.

As it turns out, Lexy has kept with the plan admirably. They went out to the porch, and, okay, they kissed awhile, but then Lexy pulled back, said she needed to talk to him about something. John, all ears: Yes? What? Sure—anything! And Lexy told him about how we needed a housemate, and how we thought he might really like the space, and seeing as he had a month-to-month lease. . . .

John was a bit surprised: She wouldn't go home with him from the bar, and now she was asking him to move in? He confessed to feeling a little confused.

Well, Lexy explained, the thing was that the finding-a-housemate thing was a higher priority than finding a boyfriend, and not that she didn't like kissing him, but if he did want to move in she felt like they'd really need to set some boundaries because what was most important to her was that Thisbe not feel left out and there was no way Thisbe was going to feel anything but left out if they kept it up if he moved in. . . .

She wouldn't have to be left out, John said.

Lexy urged him on.

John answered tentatively that, just for the record, Thisbe was sort of cute too....

Funny you should mention that, said Lexy. And then, if she hadn't already, she told him about the man with the expensive shoes and the jokes we'd made, and though she never confessed it to me she may well have told John that she knew me well enough to know when I was into somebody, and I was definitely into him.

"And once the idea was out there ...," Lexy says to me now, in my room, refreshing my wine, her wine, John's wine, wine all around! "I mean: We're young, we're healthy, how many opportunities like this come along?"

And she's right, but I think the thing that really gets us, the thing that hooks us and holds on, is the prospect of how lame we'll feel—all of us—if we back down now. We can't say no. Saying no would be like signing on for regret. And all three of us are people who can't bear that kind of regret.

"We might regret this," I remind them.

"We'd regret not doing it even more," Lexy says.

"Very true," I say. John is nodding vehemently, as though he's been forbidden to speak aloud.

"We probably need to set up some rules. Especially if John is going to move in," Lexy says, "Or not rules so much as—"

"Communication," I say. "We just have to make sure we keep talking about it—"

John interjects: "Definitely. We need to keep each other clued in, to how we're doing with it all. Like not to let anything build, resentment-wise or something. We just have to keep talking—"

"This isn't possible," I say. "Everything like this fails—"

"Yeah, but . . . ," Lexy tries.

"But," I say, "even if we're the biggest idiots on the planet—"

"We can't *not* try," John says. We are all grinning absurdly, beaming and oozing, so stupendously delighted with ourselves that there is absolutely no stopping us now.

"How much notice do you need to give them on your apartment?" I ask John.

"That shithole?" he says. "About ten minutes. They don't have a deposit or anything. Whatever. I have nothing to lose."

"So what if we try it for a little, like until you'd have to pay your next month's rent," Lexy suggests. "That'd give us a couple weeks to see how it works—"

"And time for me to get a car," John adds.

"And time to see how badly this goes," I feel compelled to chime in.

John grins at me then—the smile he'd seemed to have only for Lexy beamed right on me—as he says, "You haven't even had me yet. You'll see how unfounded that pessimism'll wind up being—"

I turn to Lexy. "He's *that* good?"

"What do I know?" she says. "All we did was kiss—"

"Well that," John says, "can be easily remedied." He leans over, his burgundy breath hot, and kisses me. One of his hands comes under my breast. The other, I see when I stop kissing back and open my eyes, is undoing the buttons of Lexy's jeans.

"Lexy's bed's more comfortable," I say, shrugging down at my paltry mattress on the floor.

"My bed it is," says Lexy. And holding hands, the three of us trot off down the hall like we're headed down the yellow brick road.

The most fabulous thing about it is that I can get up in the middle of the night and go back to my own bed, sleep alone, like I like, and wake in the morning without some big guy beside me, pressing his hard-on insistently into the small of my back. I wake up before they do, make coffee, have my time alone in the morning like I like. I am reading when I hear them getting up. Door noises, muffled talk, and then the sound of the shower going on, and I have just enough time to wonder if they're in there together when there's a knock on my door.

"Hi," says John.

"Morning," I say.

"Can I come in?"

I gesture, Sure.

He comes and sits on my bed, leans in awkwardly to kiss me. But the awkwardness dissipates as we kiss, as we remember there are no rules to this, that nothing about whatever-this-is works the way any sex, anything we've had, has ever worked before. Somehow this newness puts us all on equal footing. I have sex with John while Lexy showers, and then when she comes in, towel-wrapped and warm, they have sex too. We are going to have to replenish our condom supply. It is an amazing thing to be that close to two other people having sex. To know—and I know, because I was in their position last night—to know that they are almost as aware of me as they are of each other. As attentive to the third as to the one.

"You," Lexy says to John, when they are done, "are about the luckiest man on the planet."

"You think I don't know that?" he says, lying between us, having just come for the second time in half an hour.

"Remember that," I say.

"I could cook you breakfast," John says, "show my immense, immense gratitude."

"That'd be a start," Lexy says.

"A step in the right direction," I add.

"We can't let him get too cocky about this," Lexy says.

"I think he will probably have to be mocked mercilessly so as to be kept in line," I say.

"I think," John says dreamily, "that at this point, as far as I'm concerned, the two of you can do anything in the world you please...."

"I think," says Lexy, "that that's what all men should say to all women after they have sex."

"We're going to change the world!" John says.

"Don't get cocky," I remind him.

The next month is essentially lost to us. There is no writing for me, no painting for Lexy—we're far too busy *living!* There is not so much as a dramatic moment inked by John's pen—the poor man is exhausted! What there *is* is the moving in, the car-buying, the communicating. There is a great deal—an *admirable* deal—of *processing* among the three of us. There is much more wine, the days and nights becoming a little confused. There is whispering among friends. There is much speculation. There is much kissing. There is much sex. There is John calling up to me and Lexy from his downstairs room one morning, "Somebody? . . . Anybody? . . . I have an erection." There is me and Lexy refusing him, taunting him, prancing about in our underwear, letting him suffer. There is Lexy admitting to her old boyfriend in town that this guy—this *vegan fucking dramatist?! Lexy, you have* got *to be fucking kidding me!*—has moved into the schoolhouse under the explicit agreement that he will be sleeping with both of us. There is the old boyfriend saying, "What, Lex, are you a lesbian now?" and Lexy saying, no, not that she knows. It's not like the two of us were jumping into bed before John got there. Or the two of us jumping into bed when John's not around. "So you're bi?" asks the ex-boyfriend, determined to get this straight. "I don't know, maybe," Lexy tells him, "but it's not like we really have sex with each other, it's like either one of us with him or the other, or both of us with him but he's in the middle kind of a thing, you know?"

It takes a month for the ex-boyfriend to convince Lexy that what she really needs in her life is to get back together with him and try—for once, for the first time really try—to have a *real* relationship, not something silly or flighty or something she can run away from when things get a little sticky, but something true and lasting. No one, he tells her, will ever love her like he does. She doesn't know if he is right, but, as she tells me and John, she feels like she has to try. "What if it's true?" she says. "What if no one ever will love me like he does? I have to at least try. . . ."

"That guy sounds creepy," John says. We are in bed. We were in bed when Lexy broke the news to us. We are still in bed.

"He *is* creepy," I say. I realize this is exactly what everyone is saying about John. Probably about me and Lexy too: creepy, the whole lot of us.

"Damn," says John. "We were doing so well with this."

"I know," I say. "I was getting very proud of us. I mean, what do you do when you're the only two left in a threesome? How's that supposed to work?"

John shrugs. "But how was any of this supposed to work?" he says. "I mean, we've been making it up as we go this far—"

"I'm still having fun," I say.

"I, actually . . ." John stammers a little, "I don't know, I think I actually really kind of *like* you, you know?"

"Don't go getting soft on me," I tell him. Then, "And don't go getting cocky about it, but you're not so bad yourself after all. In my opinion—"

"Who knew you were such a romantic?" John says.

"I hide it well."

"So what are we deciding here?" he says.

"I don't know," I say, "what *are* we deciding?"

"I really don't want to move out—," John is saying, but I cut him off.

"There is no reason that you should have to move out just because she's getting back with what's his name. That would be cruel even for Lexy and me," I say.

"So you'll let me stay?" he pleads, mugging pathetic and puppy-eyed.

"Will you still sleep with me?" I ask.

"Yes, ma'am," promises John.

"You can still sleep with other people too, you know," I say. "Just so long as you're good and safe and careful. And you tell me. I like to be informed."

John holds up his Boy Scout pledge fingers. "I'll wear three condoms at once and tell you every gory detail," he swears.

"And we still get to sleep in our own rooms?"

"As you like," he agrees.

"This is becoming my ideal relationship," I say skeptically. "You're like the boyfriend I always dreamed of."

"I'll try not to let that go to my head," he says. And it doesn't.

where the boys were

~~ lily burana

For years, I've been involved with men I could never have. No need to feel sorry for me, or assume that I'm seized by some weird "women who love too much" masochism. It's just those darn gay boys. They have a permanent hold on my heart.

Their names are Kirby, Cubby, Christopher, and Jay. Kirt and Alan and Kim. They were never my lovers, but each in their own way taught me how to love.

My first gay crush was in junior high—predictably, on my hairdresser. Kirt. He had spiked hair moussed into stalagmites, smooth skin, and eyebrows tweezed to the edge of oblivion. An unspectacular-looking, reasonably charmless geek, I wasn't exactly a winner in the adolescent dating game.

But here was this sleek, solicitous man with his hands in my hair, fawning over me and giving me hope that someday, someone might find me attractive enough to claim. Haircut after haircut, trim after perm after updo, our relationship deepened. I'd never met a male so emotionally forthcoming, so interested in what I had to say. He told me he was a drag performer in his spare time, and that I was, in his estimation, a babe. I was touched by his trust in me and flattered by what I realized years later were probably just attempts to smarm me out of bigger tips. But at the time, I was besotted. I wanted to show my esteem through means beyond money, so I went out and shoplifted a pair of size twelve pumps. I presented them to him as a token of my affection, and with a grateful flutter of his lashes, our allegiance to each other was sealed.

By tenth grade, I had a hideous perm (courtesy of Kirt) and burgeoning boobs. Between my hair and my chest, I was taking up too much space altogether, and I was also prone to unfortunate fashion risks—risks that would bring me humiliation greater than a citation from the fashion police. New to radical politics and alterna-culture, I skulked the school halls with Dead Kennedys lyrics scrawled on my notebooks, a dozen silver rings in my ears, and a shredded black minidress and torn tights clinging to my rebel teen bod. I thought sneering and finger-pointing would be the worst of what my appearance might solicit until I was ambushed outside homeroom by a jock. Chris W., a greasy sophomore in sweatpants and a football jersey, came up to me one day between classes and rubbed his crotch along my thigh. He grinned like a junkyard dog and grunted with delight at my shock. I think he was pleased that he'd put me in my place:

You! Weirdo! Sex object! I still remember the feeling of his floppy little fleece-covered penis against my leg. I pushed him off me, swore mightily, and never again wore anything form-fitting to school.

Specific incidents, like terrorist humping in the hall, taught me that male sexuality could be aggressive and stupid. But it was the generalized drama of high school that clued me in to the peril of a young woman's sexual life. I learned, as every girl must, that Reputation is All, and that your reputation had less to do with what you actually did than who you did it with, as well as where and when. Your social value was externally dictated and subject to whim: If someone said you were a slut, and the gossip winds prevailed, then you were. My girlfriends and I got courted by boys and we courted back. When we found a guy we liked, we did the usual things—dated, kissed, and fooled around, and gathered to share the details later. But we were careful in how we carried ourselves publicly. On one level, we were irreverent; our poses of punky indignation stood out in our conservative school and we took to heart the lefty dictum to Question Authority. But socially, we kept to ourselves in a tight clique and toed the line when it came to advancing the requisite blank-slate sexual image. We all knew that social success was predicated upon a type of sub-mission that had nothing to do with sex, and that the straight-girl game was all image, all spin.

Maybe I was overly invested in the idea that life should be honest, but the duplicitous, rigid order of all things girl ground me down. I wore bitterness like I owned it. Knowing I couldn't fight the status quo, I ran away from it instead.

Our busy Jersey county had one little gay bar, The Yacht

Club, on a two-lane highway out by the lake. My classmate Daryl, insistent that he wasn't gay, took me out there one night, and I found an unexpected reprieve from the high school drama. Glamour wasn't on the itinerary at The Yacht Club—it was musty and dark-carpeted, and the dull parquet dance floor was ringed by secondhand captain's chairs and brass lanterns covered in fingerprints. But Daryl and I danced to Bronski Beat together and tried to get people to buy us drinks. We stumbled into the pebbled parking lot at closing time, eager to go back again. The next weekend, the bouncer turned a merciful blind eye to our obviously forged IDs, and we stepped back into what would become our one safe haven. Men outnumbered women twenty to one at The Yacht Club, and if we weren't counted as "one of the boys" because of our age and lack of gay cred, Daryl and I were at least welcome visitors. They took us in and didn't judge. Daryl wouldn't dance with a guy (yet), but I'd storm the dance floor with any guy who would ask. I started dressing outrageously for Yacht Club trips, and my recklessness was treated by the club's patrons as cause for celebration, not rebuke. I could be showy and sexy in that searching teenage way, and not have my reputation, or my spirit, whacked in return. Whatever these men wanted from me, it wasn't sex, so I felt secure. Maybe it was shallow interest in two fresh chickens, but the attention that Daryl and I received felt like a balm to me.

No one that I met at The Yacht Club was out of the closet. Every man and woman in the place kept their gayness under wraps, hinting at it only under the cover of the club's strobe-lashed darkness. But they never showed any resentment about the fact that they had to be discreet; in fact, they seemed ecstatic to have a single low-key haven in a hostile world. I guess you don't carry a chip on your shoulder when there's a friendly hand clasped there. Their largesse and gratitude in the face of having to live double lives taught me something valuable: Love and sex are vital pursuits, even if they have to be displaced, even if what you really want or do precludes full disclosure. Lots of people, for lots of reasons, have to hide some part of their loving selves—it's not just a suburban straight chick thing. This realization helped me shut down the embittered, one-person pity party I had going, and it opened me up to the possibility of love on the margins. One day, behind a divey go-go bar turned punk club, I met a boy who I became crazy about. Well, he wasn't a boy, exactly—he was a twenty-six-year-old guitar player with a mohawk and no job. I was seventeen. By now, I didn't care what anyone thought of me, thought of my choices, thought of my behavior. The fairy-dust of gay chutzpah had settled on me and solidified into something resembling armor. I thumbed my nose at the nine-year age difference and threw myself into this relationship. I stood taller, took more chances, and yet I was quieter, stealthy.

With their strongly attuned teen radar, the kids at my school knew something was up. They sniffed me for hormones and began circling for attack. Because I wasn't sexual in a way they recognized and could therefore denigrate, they couldn't quite get me with "slut," so they called me a dyke instead. I was goddamn happy about it. Sluts were utilities, meant to be passed around and passed over, but dykes were scary, to avoid at all cost. I could live with that. I remember walking past the uber-popular Angie Puccio in the mall. She muttered, "Dyke" under her breath as she sailed by. When she was ten feet past me, I yelled, "Hey, Angie!" She turned. I spread my fingers into a peace sign, put the fingers to my lips and wiggled my tongue in the crotch-like fork. She never called me a dyke, or anything else, ever again. It started then, that modus operandi, and is with me to this day: Whatever name you use to degrade me will boomerang back and get you between the eyes. When I moved to San Francisco at twenty-one, I left the margins of gay culture and dove right into its flashy, roiling center.

Like many of my female cohorts, I changed sexual orientation so much it was dizzying. My female friends and I went through a period where we fancied ourselves girl-fags—able to love as cavalierly as the gay men we idolized. After years of stifling political correctness, the yearning to break out of that collective hobble was great. We felt more than entitled to be greedy in our quest for adventure because our passion had a revolutionary grrl politik: Fun and subversion were bedmates. We tried so darn hard, thinking that it would work. Often, it didn't. We'd aim to be one-night warriors and end up falling in love. Or we'd try to be bad only to discover we'd rather just cuddle. And sometimes our misfortune was more extreme. (I will spare you the gruesome tale of the short-lived women's sex club when every grrl in town got scabies.) Like lovers of all orientations, we had our share of heartache and drama. Love thrives on tension, but sometimes it's overwhelmed by it, too. Ultimately, we learned that even though we loved gay men, we weren't good at fucking like them.

And even as a transitory queer girl, the gay boys were there. Always. Leather daddies, bears, drag queens, butch queens, faerie tops and masochist bottoms, spankers, tweakers, athletic gods and erotic geniuses—they were my friends, my allies, my role models. My women friends and I hung out at gay street fairs and leather bars, discos brimming with go-go boys, and Tenderloin all-night diners. Our roving tribe was mixed, boy with boy, girl with girl, and many variations in between.

As much as I loved my lesbian friends, I couldn't imagine not wanting to be around all that ferocious gay male energy. It was enlivening, watching how eagerly they assumed their right to pleasure. It was different than straight-boy sexual entitlement. Gay men had to work for it, overcoming the obstacles of self-loathing, isolation, and fear of attack. In other words, they had to work for it just like women. Just like me. I felt an affinity born of shared circumstances—of being at the wrong place at the wrong time. But it wasn't just a symbiosis of victimhood, either—poor me and poor you. Between a gay guy and a girl there's an indescribable spark that isn't about sexual conquest but is somehow about sex all the same. It's the eroticism of "I'm excited to know you," of basking in the glow of mutual admiration; just someone's presence generates an erotic jolt. This feeling is as intoxicating as love. There isn't any bargaining or jockeying involved, as there can be when things get physical. This is fantasyland fluff, romantic infatuation at its hilt. It's one of those things that has helped me better understand the unruliness of the heart. If someone tells me, for example, that their one-night stand was the purest love they've ever known, I nod with understanding.

The spectacle of early nineties gay male culture was not lost on me. There was something so big and fantastical about it—the clubs, the pageants, the drag (both butch and femme).

Through nightlife, they'd perfected the creation of an alternate reality, a parallel universe where love was outsized and free-flowing, and everyone looked their part, however rough or rowdy. Oppression is the father of escapism in the way that necessity is the mother of invention. Maybe that's why gay men decorate and arrange fantasy settings better than anyone. Step into their world at the right time, in the right venue, and you can believe in the Valhalla promise of eternal glory and epic fierceness, at least until closing time.

Throughout these years, I had a handful of gay men as confidants, butch leathermen every one. Some fetishized the military, others biker culture. Still others couldn't get enough of sweaty, hairy men. I found them wildly attractive, and though they only had eyes for each other, they had big arms that held me safely. I could live with unrequited urges, because more than the fleeting rush of sex, I needed what they gave me: the example of their courage; the audacity of their love.

Not one of these men is alive today. Some of them became ill and deteriorated, painfully and visibly, over the course of years. When I try to tally up the numbers, I sink into depression. Then Kim and Hal and Cubby and Kirby show up at the periphery of my thoughts and chime in that I should be happy. They gather around me and lift me up.

After my girlie phase, I drifted back toward men as romantic partners. Consider some of the men I've dated since leaving San Francisco: cowboy, construction worker, biker, army officer (who I married). It's no accident that I might as well be describing the Village People. It's Psychology 101—who you imprint upon early in your erotic life shows up later on.

I'll always have a weakness for a rock-hard man with a soft heart and a huge appetite for pleasure. I'll forever be drawn to the shine on a boot, the stiffness of a starched collar. Gender is as much of a costume drama as it is biological hardwiring, and I'm a sucker for the masculine pageant. I suppose on some level, through my choice of lovers, I've been fucking ghosts, trying to draw into me a little of what I've lost, a bit of what I couldn't have outside my dreams. We love today in the shadow of our former selves.

divisions and disparities

whereya headed?

✒ jennifer baumgardner

I read Judy Blume's *Forever* before I was ten. I was on a car trip with my parents, slouched down in the backseat of the new Oldsmobile, when I got to one of the famous pages. "What does 'I'm coming, I'm coming' mean?" I asked. I knew it was part of sex, and sexy, but it made no sense. Coming? From where? Where are you headed? It reminded me of the misleadingly active term for dating in the eighties, at least in Fargo, which was *going*, as in "I'm going with Chad." Chad was a guy who portrayed Winnie to my Kanga in the play *Winnie-the-Pooh* in 1982. We "went" together for awhile. "So, where are you two going?" my parents would tease. I don't think Chad and I ever even talked on the phone. *Going where? Nowhere.*

While going with Chad, in seventh grade, I bought a roach clip at Spencer Gifts at the Columbia Mall because I thought the purple feathers were truly beautiful. Oblivious to its real use, I wore it clipped to my dull blue ski jacket, but in bed at night I'd unclip it from the zipper and use it to tickle my abdomen, relishing the fluttering dropping feeling it elicited in my barely understood sexual regions.

From the age of six until around twelve, I was constantly touching myself at night or fantasizing about men carrying me into water. On certain special occasions never spoken of, my freckled, popular neighbor and I would play husband (me) and wife (her). We'd roll around for hours in her trundle bed with all of our clothes off, me offering little pecks to her neck and face and shoulders.

As guys began entering my life in a real way, where making out and sex were not only possible but expected, those flutters between my legs gave way to a general swollen effect from hours of making out, but no crescendo toward an orgasm. I now gleaned a bit more substantially what "I'm coming, I'm coming" was, but it was more of a dirty thing to read about in a novel than a legitimate goal of mine. By college, I was an ardent campus feminist and full of rhetoric about female sexual fulfillment (but not as much of *that* as rhetoric about date rape, coercion, the male gaze, porn's dehumanization of women, etc.). When my college boyfriend would occasionally put his mouth between my legs, I'd humor him and squirm a bit, but if he'd been a mind reader he would have understood my true feelings as "Don't bother. No, really. *Don't.*"

I wonder when I would have come if I hadn't met Anastasia. Maybe I'd still be waiting, having put off buying a vibrator, hoping to catch a fleeting orgasm as I awoke from a good dream. As it was, I was already twenty-four years old. I had been having sex ("real sex," as I thought of it, what my mom and yours call "intercourse") for just four years. My feminist years at college had blossomed into a job at *Ms.* magazine, which seemed to me to be akin to a funny guy getting a job writing for *The Simpsons* right out of college. I was in feminist hog heaven. At *Ms.* we used to joke that all of our conversations came back to food, sex, and hair, which was a relief after college, when we would have negativized that list to "bulimia, rape, and why the patriarchy forces us to shave." In addition to their love of girl-talk, the editors and designers at *Ms.* seemed to have a different relationship to orgasms than I did. They had them.

At first I thought they were lying. (Now I think people are lying when they say that they have multiple orgasms.) After a while I realized that these women—gay and straight—also masturbated, many of them, and that's how they eventually learned to come with a "partner." I listened carefully. I was interested in having an orgasm. This kind of *Our Bodies, Ourselves* discussion about how to come operates on two levels, it seems to me: *analysis* and *action*. The first part, what women *say* they do, sounds logical, as does their claim that they deserve to come—I'm all for it. Sign me up. But as far as applying their tips or advice to myself . . . well, it's sort of like hearing about how someone trained and ran a marathon or did their taxes themselves. I know it's possible and I admire that they can, but I don't think it translates to me. Besides, maybe they're lying.

So, I didn't necessarily have coming as a goal when I first

began fooling around with the soft-skinned, raven-haired, beautiful-breasted ex-*Ms.* intern Anastasia—a true bodice-ripper heroine if I ever saw one. (Except, I suppose, for her butch haircut and obsession with self-defense.) I didn't have any preconceived notions about how women made love. There was no Judy Blume book to refer to. My mind was a tabula rasa when it came to sex with a woman and I just assumed that she knew what we were doing.

She sort of did. In fact, several months after our very hot first kiss, I came. It was around noon on a Sunday in my bright studio apartment. Anastasia had this idea that we should take off all our clothes and sort of entangle our legs together so that our clitorises could touch. It sounded odd, but I thought, What the hell. We were sitting on my bed, totally naked, with the sun pouring in and frying us a little. I put my arms and legs around her and skooched in until we were all wrapped up together. There was a jolt in my body when we connected, and my first adult orgasm started me up like a car. I was so flabbergasted that I yelled, "We should patent this!" Anastasia thought people had probably done it before.

Still, she agreed it was quite an accomplishment. We were self-helpy and Wicca-ish back then. We said things like "Thank the goddess" and brushed each other's hair and took baths together. Jennifer had an orgasm! We were so pleased with ourselves that when we met her brother for brunch (a gay man who writes for television), we told him, as if he wanted to know. "Too much information," he said, back when that was funny and only fags said it. "Don't go there."

Soon, I came rather easily and often. Sometimes we'd be fully clothed, panting and kissing, scissoring our legs, when

I'd come. I loved that for some reason. Anastasia would sit up and say, "*That's* what I call safe sex." She came, I came, we all came. On it went, like that, until we broke up.

One large reason for the breakup was named Steven. He was breathtaking to me: his accent Glaswegian, his body waifish, and his mood chaotic. When he was in a good mood, I felt very appreciated and perfect and glad that someone finally got my Bob Fosse references. When he was in a bad mood, I felt like a loser and danced around trying to badger him into a good mood. With Steven, I had a lover whom people didn't assume was "just" my friend, which was a relief. Of course, we weren't such good friends, not like Anastasia and I had been, where we'd stay up all night laughing and drawing cartoons of ourselves and dreaming of publishing our own feminist zine. With Steven, though, addictive familiarity was replaced with exciting domesticity. I finally had someone I fantasized about moving in with, buying dishes with—or *for,* since he didn't have any. With Steven, the orgasms stopped.

Oddly, I didn't totally care. The fact of his coming was a not-unpleasant distraction from my own would-be orgasm. But I wasn't going to deprive myself, either. Since what I did most often with Anastasia wasn't replicable with a man, I learned to masturbate with this bootleg vibrator I fashioned out of an electric toothbrush. Eventually, I could come with my hand, as long as I was in a certain pelvic tilt position that, again, didn't seem to translate to intercourse very well. Once, early on, Steven asked me what I liked in bed. I tried desperately to come up with something to offer, but everything that crossed my mind was either a lie ("tie me up") or something better left to R. Crumb ("give me a piggyback ride"). I finally stammered my tried-and-true "I like what you do to me," but I felt lost. I didn't even know what I liked.

The girl after him? Orgasm central. Amy was sexually advanced, a real student of her own body, and a devoted lover of women. Besides, she had great breasts, which are universally understood as a good thing in sex, whether male, female, in between, straight, or gay. (I offer as proof Nancy Friday's *My Secret Garden*—the longest chapter is about straight women's fantasies about sex with women.) About the third time I slept with Amy, I orgasmed from oral sex! Being with a woman is like being Xena; the world of men suddenly doesn't matter. I opened up quickly because I trusted—or assumed—her empathy for my body and its smells and stickiness and my weird ways of getting off. Amy was sexy, talented, and the companion of my dreams: the brains of David Remnick, the body of Lara Croft, the disciplined idealism of a long-time vegetarian. But eventually, we failed, too.

Enter: Grant. Grant is a vagina expert if there ever was one. He is a dedicated reader of both Rimbaud and of magazines that feature bleached blondes with waxed assholes and their legs over their heads. He knows who Butt Man is; he is well-versed in his considerable oeuvre. When I shared with him Naomi Wolf's *Beauty Myth* conceit that women resent porn because "it makes them feel ugly in sex"—meaning they don't want to be compared with the perfection and compliance of a porn star—he replied, "But *porn* is ugly." (And he's right. No one who makes it in porn is gorgeous enough to even appear in a maxi pad commercial. It is not the site of idealized beauty.) "Besides," he added, "sex isn't pretty."

Despite the fact that his cupboards are filled not with

plates and boxes of pasta but with red plastic cassettes, I feel that yummy domestic feeling again with Grant, just as I did with Steven. Within days of our first kiss, I daydreamed about moving in with him: Grant cooking breaded chicken breasts while I folded laundry. The fact that he invests in a collection of overpriced tapes featuring women accommodating too much (probably in order to buy diapers) doesn't convey Grant's appeal, especially his sex appeal, but the guy has it. He has it the way a lesbian has it—he *loves* women's bodies. He cries when I put my underwear on; he sleeps with his face on my abdomen, nose tickled by my pubic hair. I bought sheer underwear because I was so amazed by his jaw-dropped response. His erections still shock me, emerging between his skinny hips at the drop of a hat.

With Grant, I do stuff I never dreamed of—sex on tables, in bathrooms, in showers, at friends' houses, with not a moment to spare, while wearing a taffeta dress, in the 110-degree heat. Right off the bat, I felt like I could possibly come with him. Do I? Well . . . I can now come with him and a vibrator happening at the same time. And in a somewhat romantic gesture, he has purchased quite a few gifts for me at Toys in Babeland—but it's a lot of work.

Now, I know what you're thinking. You're thinking, This woman is gay. She should stick with women. I've thought that—and tried that—but I am drawn significantly to men. Given the problems associated with male partners (my short list includes snoring, inability to make a bed, terrifying relationships with their mothers), let's assume that I wouldn't try if I didn't feel like I really wanted them. Besides, just as I want gay people to have the same rights and privileges as straight people, I want straight people to have the same privileges of equality and freedom from gender-role expectations that gay people often have. In plain English: I want to have orgasms with my partners, regardless of their gender. More specifically, right now, I want to have an orgasm with Grant. Grant sans vibrating pink rubber thing.

Thinking back to *Forever,* it's the protagonist's boyfriend, Michael, who announces that exciting couplet, "I'm coming. I'm coming." I don't think anything happens for our hero Kathy other than helping him mop up the sperm on her stomach after his climax. How apt that she was my first sexual heroine. If she were an in-the-flesh friend of mine, what would she say to me? *Hey, at least you have orgasms with girls!* I know, I would answer, but I'm with him now.

There remain two conflicted sides of me—the girl who can come and the girl he comes with—and they are not yet, may never be, one. My sex life is the halfway point, not the end, of a you-go-girl feminist-y book. "Baby," Grant says, trying to reassure me, "you've come a long way."

the so-called wife

eo amy keyishian

R emember *thirtysomething*? I hated that fricking show. I
didn't understand the lives of these settled, boring, older
people, and I especially didn't get why Melanie Mayron, the
lone single girl of the whole angst-ridden crew, was treated
like such a pariah. She flitted—well, dive-bombed—from man
to man, and her biological clock could have had its own spin-
off on Thursday nights. I knew it was wrong. And yet I was
riveted. Young as I was, I lived in constant fear of ending up
like her character: interesting and unlovable. To this day I de-
test the production team of Herskovitz and Zwick (despite *My
So-Called Life*) for warping my gooey young mind and teaching me to equate singledom, specifically unmarried-dom, with
desperation and kookiness.

Hence my marriage. And since I did a nice thing for a stupid reason, hence, also, my divorce.

My family had no inkling my marriage would be such a disaster. I pulled the wool over their eyes for a long time. Come to think of it, I pulled it over my own eyes, too. And my ex-husband's. Actually, if I'm going to be honest, my entire three-year state of matrimony was an extended exercise in wool-pulling in the ocular vicinity. I'm surprised the wedding pictures didn't show* us all wearing navy watch-caps and bumping into things.

Well, that's not entirely true. The fact is—and this is a fact that I had forgotten until recently—I had my doubts from the beginning. I loved J. Loved him like . . . a brother. Oops.

I met J. in college, when I was a party girl and he was the safe guy I'd sit with while deciding what completely unsuitable dude I'd be scamming on that evening. He was that cliché we'd all like to pretend we never said: "too nice." It took me years, and the gaining of some thirty pounds, to walk away from my parade of unacceptable bad boys and finally say yes to his advances. I felt like Molly Ringwald if she settled down with Jon Cryer instead of Andrew McCarthy at the end of *Pretty in Pink*.

There was nothing wrong with J. He had all the necessary attributes of a good boyfriend: ponytail, goatee, flannel shirt, Navarro-like guitar skills, membership in a popular college band that was written up in *Rolling Stone*. But for some reason, it didn't add up to sexy for me. There was some essential chemistry missing between us. There was no "click."

I smugly justified—to myself, and actually, to anyone who asked—the lack of click. I said, "Do you know what that click is? It's the sound of your brain turning off." Secretly, though, I wondered if this bizarre logic had any basis in reality. When I asked my therapist if maybe I should feel more, I dunno, *oomph* about him, she scoffed, saying she'd watched me go through enough emotional upheaval in my life. "It's time to grow up," she said. I decided she was right. So, clickless, I wed—just in time for my becoming-thirtysomething cutoff.

Things were great for about a year. This is when I did some of my best wool-pulling. "Married sex is better than any other kind," I insisted. I told my friends it was the safest I had ever felt. The security went beyond "there's someone in my bed, holding me." I had created a new family. We were each other's, now. We answered to us, not to my parents, nor to his. On Thanksgiving, *we* chose where we'd go; our parents no longer felt the need to stake their claim on us. In fact, all parental flak was gone. Their job was done.

The trouble was, I had a nagging voice telling me, Yeah, the sex is cozy and warm, but there is something missing. "Sure, there's something missing," I told the voice. "Tears. Desperation. Unhappiness. Now shut up." But as I used my newfound security as impetus to lose weight, get a better hair-cut, shave my armpits, and move up professionally, I found myself *ack*ing.

In an early Woody Allen movie called *Love and Death*, Diane Keaton has an extended monologue in which she asks herself if she can marry the nerdy cousin who's been pursuing her since childhood. "Suffocated! Can't breathe! *Ack!*" she says as she imagines her future with him. "Open a window! No, no, not that one—the one in the bathroom!"

I started to worry that my husband, whom I was putting

through graduate school, would never be able to earn a living. The future as I saw it consisted of endless moves from small academic village to small academic village, hoping for a tenure-track position. I heard of other philosophy students who studied chaos theory and made a killing advising Wall Street types, but when I brought it up, I was laughed out of the living room. I remembered growing up in an academic family, stretching dollars until George Washington looked like Alfred E. Newman. I saw myself with a stack of pennies pinched between my fingers, and I didn't like it. I began to get mean. J. retreated into the world of the Knicks and the World Cup. I developed passionate crushes on anyone without a goatee or a flannel shirt. And the sex, comfortable as it was, went out the window.

"It doesn't matter, everybody says there's no sex after babies anyway," I told my sister, who stared back at me with dumbfounded horror. "So once I have one, the sex won't be an issue." She smiled and patted me on the shoulder, unsure of what to say.

Eventually, things went kablooey. The month we were scheduled to start trying to make a baby, I saw a woman with a kid in a stroller, using her finger to fill a straw with juice and empty it into the waiting maw of her needy child. Something in the gesture was so weary, so bored, so repetitive that it gave me a panic attack. First I felt nausea. Then I began to experience a constant, speedy feeling, as if I had drunk a liter of caffeine after popping a No-Doz. It started that day and it never seemed to end. And it got worse when I went home. Something simply wasn't right, and no position I rolled into made it go away. Within days, I announced the marriage was over. We tried counseling, but even in the earth-toned therapist's office I was fidgety, sweaty, glancing constantly at the door. I told the nice therapist that I just wanted out, now, right now, immediately, and he had to help me get out. Now. When J. asked me how he could give me what I wanted, I had no answer, just glared at him with the fury and embarrassment of a thirteen-year-old whose father wears the wrong pants to pick her up at the mall. I felt disgusting. The memory makes me convulse with regret. But some horrible part of me wouldn't stop. I had to get away. And until the door shut behind J. as he removed the last of his stuff, I kept acting out: avoiding him, coming home late, lying about anything and everything—basically, just acting as disgusting as possible so he wouldn't feel so bad about losing me.

Most people, including my parents, were shocked and horrified. Some friends deserted me entirely, dismissing me as hopelessly selfish (but more flabbergasted, I suspect, that I'd given up the holy grail they were still chasing). Some gazed at me, with that *I am really trying to be supportive, but don't you remember the night you flipped out in the bathroom of Wetlands because you smoked too much Chronic and saw your future as utterly devoid of anyone who'd settle down and make babies with you so you wouldn't have to go out to slimy hippie clubs anymore and pretend to like bad music?* look on their faces, and said, instead, "Well, I'm sure if you're doing this, you must have a really good reason." And a few said, "Phew."

That core few, the Hardcore Four as I now call them, were my close posse from college. And they told me about an event I'd totally blocked from my mind.

They'd walked into the pre-wedding view-the-bride room,

where I was sitting in a voluminous white dress trimmed with beaded flowers, twisting my lace-gloved hands into a knot as I tried to sit very, very still. My hair was styled in a way they liked, but had never seen before: glossy banana curls tumbling around my face. They had been the only ones to predict the dress I would choose. "She tries to be a rebel but can't wait to put on that white gown," Tina had said, presciently, years earlier. All that was fine. It was my expression that bothered them. . . .

Think about that old cliché "so-and-so looked like a deer caught in headlights." Verbal wallpaper, right? Now picture this: A deer is grazing on a quiet country road at night. A car comes around the bend at fifty miles per hour. The deer looks up. Sees the light. Gazes into it. Becomes mesmerized. Her eyes widen. It's sudden, flashy, overwhelming, and she can't tear her eyes away. Rather than bounding into the brush where she'd be safe, she stays stock-still, her mind void of anything but the light.

That's what I looked like. Only it wasn't a Pathfinder coming at me. It was a husband. A nice, safe, normal husband. What was my problem?

"I can't move," I'd sputtered the minute they walked into the room. "What am I doing here? Can I be with him for the rest of my life? Pam—" I clutched Pam's arm like it was the only available hanging strap on a runaway D train. "You used to be a big whore. What's it like being married? Is it okay? Can I be faithful?"

"It's fine," she said, giving me a supportive smile. "It's like a lifelong experiment in monogamy. You have freedom to try anything with each other. Because you're safe." Full disclosure: Pam dumped her husband two years later and ran off with a hot-blooded labor organizer.

I sat there, wide-eyed. My friends traded glances, worried. But what could they do? The day was upon us—it was too late to sneak me out the back door and drive me to Atlantic City. Besides, I wasn't marrying Dennis Rodman. J. was a nice guy. Maybe, they hoped, this was a momentary lapse. They made burbling, supportive noises and hoped for the best, drowning their worries later that night and never bringing up my outburst until four years later, when we were all at the beach in North Carolina, my experiment in committed monogamy over and done with.

My mom just had one request, when I met her at the Museum of Modern Art, a few days after I'd made my final decision, to try to explain what in God's name I was doing. "Just don't latch on to someone unacceptable," she said. "Don't leap on the next man that comes your way. Take time to be single if that's what you want."

But it was too late. And *unacceptable* is a relative term. That night, I stretched out next to a man whose very scent turned my brain into scrambled eggs and made my skin itch to be touched by him, in the bucket seat of his sedan, parked by the East River, watching the stars shining not just through the sky-grime of New York but through the tint in his moonroof. I'd just given him a Francis Bacon book that I'd bought in the MoMA gift shop. He pulled me under him and flicked a switch, opened a faucet, gave me the wonder-twins-activate-*ka-blam* touch that turned me back into the juicy, sultry, musky, receptive-and-responsive creature that I had almost forgotten about.

"I'm back," I whispered.

"Where'd you go?" he asked.

"I dunno. Never mind," I answered, smelling his hair, feeling like I wanted to say everything they said in the romance novels I hated (but sometimes wrote, when I needed a few bucks): That I'd been dying on the vine; that he filled me with a tidal wave of lust; that I ached for him in a way I'd thought was behind me; but that it was better than everything behind me, because our coupling worked on every level, emotional and physical and even intellectual. . . . Nah. Better to keep quiet for now.

It's been five years, and the florid romance writer in me is still having her wonder-twin powers activated by Mister Faucet. So far, I haven't lost myself, nor have I felt the need to collect evidence that I should be alone again. I'm not quite married—I don't get half his fortune if we split. Nor do I automatically get the house (house! not apartment!) if he drops dead. (Astonishingly, my own greatest fear is no longer my own death, but his.) But I no longer tie my sense of financial security to my relationship, anyway. I suspect my terror of living a pauper's life with J. was more about waking up one day with a small heart than with a small bank account.

Still, it has to be pointed out that the safety is utterly gone. The mapped-out future has been replaced with uncertainty. The parental approval has been supplanted by shock and dismay. I realized that the would-be baby had been a kind of shorthand to me. The same way that certain people moon over their first dose of LSD, others talk about the miracle of breeding: that it opens you up, that it makes you whole. Yet I see too many miserable mothers avoiding, mistreating, or ignoring their kids to believe that it's the magic bullet to full womanhood. I really don't think it's for me. Instead of wishing for the perfect little child to make me a woman, I'm looking, still always looking, for ways to be myself, to feel whole, to continue to evolve and create and nurture outside the neat cookie-cutter construct of marriage, baby, home.

Who knows. Maybe Mister Faucet will go down the drain, or I'll end up Gloria Steinem-ing it at sixty-five. In the meantime, I'm enjoying my thirty-somethings. My life seems to want to take on its own shape. And for now, I prefer uncertainty to inertia.

plot vs. character

⤳ quinn dalton

He's the only guy I ever met at a bar and then took to bed. He was twenty-nine and in town from Baltimore for the summer, overseeing the renovation of the old courthouse, living out of a Holiday Inn. I was twenty-one, a broadcast cinema major with an acceptance letter in my back pocket from a film school in England for a year of study. I was celebrating. He bought me a drink and asked whether I knew the bar we were in was once the town's cathouse. He was tall and lean and green-eyed, but not pretty—nose had maybe been broken, chipped front tooth, some nice wear and tear. Smiling, yet very serious about his history lesson. He stamped the floor. "Solid," he said.

Kissing him on what occurred to me was a rather rickety

footbridge over the river, I realized I was with what appeared to be a grown man. Compared to the beer-slugging, monosyllabic fratheads comprising the college selection, he was good with words, good with his hands. I decided to trust him not to kill me, and took him to my place.

For the rest of the summer, we went to bad movies, then to the river's edge, and had sex so hard our bodies turned nearly 360 degrees on the blanket. Sometimes I went to his hotel room, but he liked it best outside, and I found I did too. "I enjoy a little dirt in my hair," he said, and I obliged, pressing his shoulders into the damp ground.

At summer's end there was no breakup, just the two of us wrapped in a polyester bedspread on the concrete slab balcony outside his room, his breath still coming hard, hands on my hips, as he told me he couldn't believe I was leaving. Of course, he was leaving, too. But this was part of his appeal, how he could appear to be heartbroken when this was not in fact the case. And I fell for it—for him. I'll just admit that now.

I went to England, distracted myself with red-cheeked British boys, came home, graduated, and took a job with a small video production company, where I edited low-budget corporate presentations, commercials, product demos, and the occasional soap opera episode. He became the story I told my friends. I said, trying to sound nonchalant, "The best thing about it was we knew how it would end."

But of course I should've known better, right? How does knowing the end help anything? There are women who would've moved on from this as neatly as a housewife trades out her old detergent when a new brand comes along. I've met these women, but I could never be one of them, try as I might.

Here's the truth about me: I am a clingy sort, mourning old toothbrushes and my stuttering TV, things that beg retirement. I tried the usual strategies—working a lot, rearranging my apartment furniture—but inevitably my mind rolled to the builder like a marble on a slanted floor. The feeling emerged like hunger, or being too cold, and usually at the end of the evening, after I'd gone from work to gym to errands to the freezer for another prepackaged dinner.

Eventually, a fantasy took shape. It went like this: A location shoot takes me to Baltimore, where the builder lives, still single. We have dinner. He invites me back for a long weekend (but now, looking back, I wonder why *I* had to come to *him*, even in the fantasy). There are sizzling nature walks in the Shenandoah Valley. We get married.

Here's what really happened. A year passed. I got back from a location shoot in Atlanta, and there was a voice mail from Baltimore. The builder was in Winston-Salem for the weekend, pitching new business. He took me to dinner at a restaurant in a historic inn, and we sat in the candlelit garden room with floor-to-ceiling open windows. He was still lean and well-muscled, yet he also looked older, tired around the eyes, which for some reason made me want to exhaust him further. He looked at me as if he might pull me with him to the floor at any moment; instead he tipped back his chair and stroked the wainscoting with a fingertip. The message was clear: *This fingertip wants to trace your lines too, honey.*

How *done* this was, really, the long gaze, then the eyes averted, as if he was frightened by his desire. If you outlined the average soap episode, which I unfortunately did often, for pay, you'd see at least three of these loaded stares, and not more than five, in forty-four minutes. And yet I must admit how well it worked on me. After we ate, he insisted on walking to my car. When he took me in his arms in the parking lot, I froze like a netted rodent, heart flicking in my throat, wondering what he would do next. But the builder was interested in an innocent full-body hug, of which he determined the closeness and the duration. I drove away, still clinging to certain notions about the smart, carefree woman I wanted to believe I was. It was a conflicting persona, though. The carefree woman would sleep with a man because she wanted to; the smart woman knew her limits, and this man somehow exceeded them.

Why? Here's what I knew about the builder, which is to say, what I'd started to suspect about myself: I was in love with him. Or the idea of him, which strongly featured the dual characteristics of handiness and a love for modern literature (well, he'd hinted at reading Hemingway and had asked me if he should dare to eat a peach once, but I think he'd been talking about something other than the paralysis of desire). He was an image to me, not exactly a man. I knew this, but knowing it didn't make me want him any less.

Nevertheless, when he called the next day I showed up, and—surprise—he led me up a shady trail above the Blue Ridge Parkway. It was sunny but humid from recent rain; I watched him wind through rhododendron and I got all confused, turned on by the smell of wet earth. Then dinner again; I was so hungry that I was sweating, and my legs were wobbly from all those slippery inclines. I was exhausted, but when he suggested a movie I heard myself saying yes. What was the movie even about? I don't know—there was a green dress, a blown-up car, subtitles. But I did know the story line from there: the arm sliding around my shoulders, the voice dropping to a whisper, all that nutritious blood my brain needed draining straight to my crotch.

Back at his hotel room, I realized I had no idea if he had a home, or if that leather bag on the luggage stand, the same one he'd had two years ago, was all there was. He laid me on the bed fully clothed, took his shirt off. I could feel how hard he was as he pressed down on me again.

The phone rang, so loud that we both jerked away from each other, startled. He sat up, answered it, listened for a moment.

"Maribel," he said. I sat up, cheeks hot, nipples hard, underwear soaked. *Maribel?* Who the fuck was that? Who had a name like that anymore? Oh, I could see her—she was small-boned and dark-haired; she blushed easily and owned pottery. I wanted him to say he'd call her back—because it was too much to ask the gods for him to say, *I thought you understood it's over; I've found who I want*—and right then I realized that for all my fantasizing, I'd really been waiting for this one scene. I needed dramatic tension, and there we were.

He was hunched forward, elbows on his knees, one palm propping up his forehead, the other clutching the phone. Not even an apologetic glance my way. *Get up get up!* I screamed at myself, but I was still sitting there, straining to hear her voice, trying to figure out what she was saying that had such power over him.

"You fucked me," he said then. "You fucked me over." Not an accusation, a complaint begging consolation. I managed to swing my legs over the edge of the bed, my toes digging into the worn carpet, searching for balance. "Wait," he said, turning to me when he felt the bed shift as I pushed myself to my feet. He reached for me, missed.

I slid on my shoes. "Look," he said, "I'll call you back." He hung up. So I got my wish, right? He said he'd call her back! Some victory.

"Is that your wife?" I managed to ask. I knew to keep going for the door; he'd follow. It was in every script: Chick runs stage right crying [*holds damp hankie*]; guy runs after her [*wears lipstick-stained shirt and rumpled pants*]. I had entered one of my own productions.

"Please come here," he said.

I knew this one. I was cued for my line: "Don't. I don't want to hear it."

"Just sit with me for a few minutes. I know you're going to go."

Tugging on my hand, he led me back to the bed. I allowed this to be enough persuasion to sit. I wasn't even sure I could drive. I was too exhausted, drunk, turned on. And another part of me, distant as a moon, orbited the planet that was myself, curious. What would he say? What would I do?

"I'm sorry," he said. Sticking with the script so far. He turned to me. Was he going to kiss me? I was about to laugh. But no, he hugged me, and this was worse. It was the breakup scene I thought I'd avoided. This ruined him as a good story, the one that made me look sexy, confident, free. It erased a future plotline I thought might be available to me. From then on, he could only be a flashback.

He slid his hands up the back of my shirt, talking into my hair, which I love. When he said he'd always felt he had to treat me with kid gloves because I was so young, I couldn't even raise an eyebrow and tell him to go back to his makeup trailer. *Up, up, up!* I could hear my muscles shrilling, but I let him hold me until he was ready to let go, and as I walked to the door, I knew there wouldn't be any speeches to stop me.

An unexpected scene a month later: hallway of the low-ceilinged office building where I work. Guy in suit stands in front of the open double doors of the suite next to mine—heavy black-chrome eighties décor within—talking on a cell phone. I realize there's a pattern: guy in hallway, me passing, small talk, repeat. That morning he gives me his card, then asks me out. This is a new one.

The following Friday evening: a Japanese restaurant, warm and rainy outside; candlelit table, funny waiter is generous with sake. Guy looks better out of the suit. Brown hair, wide-set brown eyes, not too tall but taller than me. He tells me he's an engineer. I ask him if they still give out those striped caps. He laughs. He takes me home, the two of us sit on my bare wood floor and listen to music. I keep my distance because now I don't trust myself; my carefree persona bit it that night in the hotel in Winston-Salem. She died young, barely formed, and now I'm an alcoholic at a martini bar when it comes to men; I have no judgment. This is what I've come to believe. When he leaves we're both playing it so cool we nearly shake hands.

The next morning, the phone wakes me, but I miss the call. I dial voice mail, and who could it be but the builder with the cinematic sense of timing, taking my breath away with his casual hello? I call him back that evening, eager to keep a wounded but still vigorous fantasy alive. Of course, this all against my better judgment. Somewhere in my mind there resides a delicate connection with reality that knows I won't be satisfied. But the body remembers its desires long after they make any sense. You recite the old motions. Just like riding a bike.

So first, I prepare: a few glasses of wine, some jazz. By the time I call him, I think I *am* Billie Holiday. The builder tells me it's over between him and Maribel the potter. I don't miss a beat; I ask when he'll be in town next. He's not sure.

Then it comes to me, seeping somehow through the snowy static of alcohol and hopefulness I've wrapped myself in. A moment of clarity: I know there's nothing I can say. Eventually I'll forgive myself my desires. So I tell him to let me know when he is sure, and hang up. I don't know if I'll hear from him again, but I do know this: The builder is interested in my admiration only so much as it feeds his ego. I can tell he's lonely, maybe a little desperate to know what his future holds—will he get married? Have children? Perhaps he wants these things, but not with me, that much is clear.

A week later. Sharing a six-pack with the engineer on the grass next to the retention pond behind his apartment building, watching the moon rise, just shy of full. This town is prickly with new complexes with names like Duck Run and Fox Hollow. He has no furniture. I ask about it. He asks me where mine is. I say, "I like the minimalist look." I don't tell him I never bought much because without realizing it I had been preparing for a move that wasn't going to happen. He nods. He's scared to kiss me; I know this. It used to turn me off, shyness in men, but now I like it. I decide I can wait for him to work up his courage.

Of course, there's one more message. The builder says he wants to "continue our previous conversation," which probably means he'll tell me he's not sure he wants me, but he'll say it in a way that will allow me to translate it into possible affection. My salvation is that I won't settle for it.

And what will not settling mean? This is fresh territory, a room so new I can smell the cut wood and drying plaster. I test the floor, open a window. Throw the script out, one page at a time.

my year of missed connections

෴ mikki halpin

I 've always been obsessed with the "Missed Connections" ads in newspapers. Not every paper has them, but the alternative weeklies usually do, squished in the personals somewhere between Discreet Activity Partners and the rather thrilling Anything Goes. You can also find them on websites like nerve.com, craigslist.org, and others that offer free posting space to the single, tech-savvy, and bi-curious. There are thousands of new MC posts every day, and if I could read them all, I would. Each one encapsulates a little saga of fate, hope, and the romantic desire for a second chance at love:

MC at the anarchist bookstore on East Seventh, last Monday.
You: short haired, in a Tori Amos T-shirt. Me: wearing glasses

and a STEAL THIS T-SHIRT T-shirt. You had some amazing insights about Chomsky. Sadly, the ring of the cash register ended our conversation (damn capitalism!). To continue our dialectic, answer this ad at Box 354.

Will the short-haired girl ever get in touch with the meta–T-shirt guy? What if she doesn't see the ad? What if she spills coffee on it? What if her mean boyfriend sees it and then hides the paper? What if someone else answers by mistake? What if she thinks it's utterly bourgeois? Will these little anarchists ever find true love?

Of course, I do not scan the Missed Connections solely because I take an interest in the romantic lives of my fellow citizens. Truth be told, I mostly scan them hoping to see an ad that I will come to realize, slowly and humbly, is about *moi*. I haven't yet come across one describing a girl with green eyes, wearing a sweater covered with cat hair, glaring at people on the subway, but it could happen. When I remember, I force myself to stop glaring and sometimes even chat up total strangers in the hopes that they will place an ad seeking me, but it still hasn't happened. Once or twice I have gone so far as to chat someone up, and then casually introduce the subject of the Missed Connections section, thereby—subtly—planting the seed of how to get in touch with me.

I did this even when I was with my last boyfriend, although I loved him and would never have answered an ad that was looking for me. Well, unless it was from him. I dropped a lot of hints, hoping he'd have the bright idea to place one and set up some sexy rendezvous, but he broke up with me instead. Fucker.

The first thing I did after the breakup was call up all my girlfriends for an emergency meeting. They brought over chocolate and Kleenex, listened to me cry, talked me out of getting more cats, and did all the things you are supposed to do when caring for the brokenhearted. I was content to let this phase of the recovery go on indefinitely; I love chocolate and was fairly sure that if I only left my house to go to the movies, I would never have to accept the breakup, thereby eliminating the need to ever begin dating again. Besides, being alone had its advantages. I didn't miss shaving my legs or listening to Leonard Cohen. My friends had other ideas. No, that's not true. They had one other idea: that I had to "get back out there." The thought of asking someone on a date terrified me. The thought of getting set up on a date was even worse. There was only one thing to do: connect with a missed connection of my own. So I placed my first ad:

MC New Year's Eve Day 2002, at the 2:20 P.M. showing of *Die Another Day*.

You: dark haired, with two friends who seemed to be a couple. Me: freshly single, in a yellow wool coat. You looked at my popcorn and fries and moved over, thinking I must have a date because of all that food, but I didn't! I just couldn't decide! I figured, I'm single now, why not treat myself. Then I thought, Maybe he feels the same way. E-mail me and we could meet for a matinee and carbs. No pressure.

P.S. I hope you agree with me that Halle Berry is totally not a Bond girl. I mean, she's hot, but she's so good and pure and nice. She doesn't have that nasty edge that Bond girls should have. Her name in the movie was "Jinx!" I was expecting it to be "Caramel Buns" or something. Feh.

Perhaps out of some misplaced loyalty to Halle Berry, he didn't answer. But that didn't stop me. I began leaving the house more and more—not really to meet people, but to give myself reasons to place more ads:

MC at Ethan's birthday party, January 24, Niagara bar, 11 P.M.

You: tall, blond Ivy League–educated hipster. Me: satin dress (not desperate-for-attention satin, nice satin), tattoos. Last night we had about twenty drinks each and a long discussion about obscure eighties bands (BTW you are totally wrong about Hetch Hetchy). I haven't had sex in months and boy, I thought you were going to get lucky!!! Imagine my surprise and disappointment when you looked at your watch and told me you had to go pick up your girlfriend after her shift at Scores. But hey, maybe you've gotten tired of her. And you know what? I'm not ready for anything serious anyway! I just got *out* of a relationship, remember? I'm only looking for some fun, dude. You know the number.

MC at Ruth's opening, mid-March, Andrew Kreps Gallery in Chelsea, 8-ish.

Me: in a Balenciaga knockoff. You: an orange windbreaker and cords. We seemed to have about a zillion friends in common, and I loved making fun of that preppy guy with you. You're the only guy who has ever made me laugh as much as my ex, and you have better hair. I loved how you got me drinks at all the openings we hit afterward and how you want to have kids. (I don't, actually, but maybe I would for you.) I've already figured out how my cat and your dogs will get along. I don't even mind that you are gay! My friends keep telling me I should be open to new types of guys (let's just say there's been a dry spell). Let's do it! My profile is on Friendster and there is a secret encoded message to you within it.

As the year went on, I learned a lot about what dating experts like to call "mixed messages." I even sent some of my own:

MC with hot young cartoonist, June 27, loft party in Chelsea.

Me: burned-out older woman on the verge of bitter. You: fresh out of college in the Midwest, unaware of what a hot commodity you are in NY. You showed me your comics, and called me every night for months. I couldn't deal. For all my Mrs. Robinson fantasies, for the love of Ashton and Demi, I just couldn't do it. Let's face it, I still really love that same guy I was dating when I met you. But I could get over him at any time! And not to lead you on, but the phone calls were nice. Could you start them up again? Thanks. No promises.

That guy never saw the ad, but he did start calling me again, and I immediately blew him off again because I was too busy obsessing over my ex. This made my friends angry. They accused me of always wanting what I couldn't have, ignoring a total hottie, and possibly harboring secret plans for more cats. They were right. Especially about the first thing.

MC August 9, at the Siren Festival, Coney Island.

Me: covered in sunscreen and really cranky about the heat. You: charming as usual, and I'm going to overlook the Wilco T-shirt. It was nice to see a familiar face in the crowd, even if it was you, O elusive boy. I wonder if by now you're over that whole fake boob stripper thing and you are ready to date someone like me—less showy but actually with quite big boobs that I came by naturally! I did see you getting on the subway with an Alyssa Milano look-alike, but I think she was just a friend. I guess I'll know for sure if you reply.

I never found out if his heart was with me or Alyssa Milano, but it was probably better that way. Reality isn't really the point in the world of Missed Connections: Why do you think I liked it there so much? It was a world where romantic optimism wasn't a death sentence.

MC every morning at 8:30, the L Café, Williamsburg.

The first time I came in, you looked kind of pissed off as you asked me if I wanted my iced Americano in a large or a medium cup. But I couldn't help noticing how cute you look when you are annoyed. Plus, I am sure your job is stressful. I'm currently in the process of exploring things with younger guys, so if the age thing doesn't bother you, it's cool with me! I see us as partnering through bohemia, making zines and agitprop art, starting a band, and having lots of stoop sales to make rent. We'll get all hopped up on free coffee from your job and repaint our living room to match the sunset, then split a can of beans and go to sleep holding hands. Give me an extra shot in my next drink, and I'll get the message.

MC with a pedicab driver, corner of Fortieth and Broadway, Oct 10.

Me: desperately trying to get to some stupid party at the Friar's Club. You: muscley, sweaty, able to see through all that. I'm sorry I wouldn't get into your cab. I felt that doing so would start our relationship off on a note of inequality. I loved how you wouldn't take no for an answer though! Persistence is sexy. And I'm guessing a pedicab driver is pretty good with his hands. I need some shelves put up, and I've never had a boyfriend who could do anything like that. I could also use some help fixing my door. I have a tendency to live inside my head, so this relationship will be great for me—lots of fresh air and just good, practical views on life. God I hope you have a computer, or you'll never see this! You aren't totally living an anti-techno lifestyle are you? I guess I'll know when you answer this ad.

MC at the Friar's Club, October 10.

Me: in an evening poncho and jeans, soaking wet (I had to walk there) and trying to figure out which of the party guests were *New Yorker* writers. You: tall, witty, reading from your sure-to-be-a-bestseller book. You're cute! And self-deprecating, I love that. The last guy I liked worked in transportation, so your braininess is a total attraction. Together we can take the literary world by storm. We could be the Stiller and Meara of words! (Because I'm Irish and you're Jewish!) I suspect you are married, but if not, have your agent call my agent.

But after almost a year of imagining happy endings for myself, I felt a change. I began to wonder why I was wasting my time with Missed Connections when I was still feeling one particular *connection* very strongly. This is the last ad I ever placed:

MC with my ex, December 20, 2002, exactly 345 days after we broke up.

I know, I know, it was just a one-night encounter. We aren't back together. Yeah, you love me and I love you but we aren't back together. We miss each other, but we aren't back together. The sex is still good, but we aren't back together. We laugh a lot, but we aren't back together. Please don't call me. If you want to reach me, you know where I'll be looking. I'll be looking every day.

hiding the kid

ᵕᵒᵕ lisa carver

headed out for my date already tired, even though it was only
two in the afternoon. I was tired because my day had begun
ten hours earlier, at 4 A.M. with my three-year-old's nightmare
about a red moon blowing. I was leaving for a date so early because it was a six-hour drive away, in New York. It was the
fourth of July, and getting stickier in my unair-conditioned,
dented Geo Metro, which could get up to one hundred miles an
hour and was exempt from being pulled over (I think they felt
sorry for me and let me have my little bit of happiness in the
form of unticketed rushing about). I didn't know anything at all
about my date—which my friend Kate was arranging—except
that it involved at least one adult male penis. A grown-man
penis that wouldn't pee the bed or have to be put in the tub or

yelled at should its owner drop his pants as a prank on the neighbor lady. No, I wasn't responsible for this unknown penis in any way, shape, or form. All I had to do was allow it to give me joy and happiness, and then I'd get away before finding out about anything attached to that penis, like emotions.

I arrived at the club, and my good, blond, alcoholic friend (all single moms need one of these) pointed out the three sleazy guys from whom I was to choose. Her gift to me was this lineup of her slutty yet kind male friends, all in bands. She knew I was weighed down by being solely in charge of someone with a vocabulary of only fifty words, and really, physically weighted down by carrying the thirty-pound beast when he got all nappy. I was starting to feel permanently bent by the sheer repetition of strapping him in and out of his car seat, leaning over to feed and clean and change and feed and explain yet again why we don't stick our fingers into electrical outlets. My good, blond friend had come up with this scheme to make me light again, to unbend me.

Because single motherhood requires intense coordination and speed at all tasks, I was able to make my choice right away and with perfect rightness: the one who was skinniest, with white wings bleached into his black pompadour, sipping a root beer nice and slow. Everything was already understood, and within a minute of meeting, we were making out. Within an hour, we were in his room in an apartment of rock boys, on his bunk bed, which felt to me as thin and as high as a magic carpet. He was a professional lover, a mechanic so skilled that, were I looking at him as a potential boyfriend, I would have felt nervous and jealous of all the—I'd guess—four billion women he'd had before me. That would be my highly accurate estimate. As it was, I simply felt grateful. He administered trick after gasket-tightening trick until I do believe a light the color of butter started shining from all my orifices—that's how happy I was.

At one point I sat bolt upright and said, "Where did you learn that?"

"Learn what?"

"That thing, what you just did!"

"Oh, uh. An instructional video."

He resumed performing the thing upon me that I didn't understand, and I had this thought that should have been creepy but instead felt good and right: *He's mothering me!* He'd done research (watching the instructional video)! He was here to take care of me, to discern needs I couldn't name and to be responsible for how they were met. Suddenly, "I love you!" popped out of my mouth. I didn't even know his real last name (just his rock one). But why shouldn't I have loved him? Does love need to last forever to be true? I didn't feel self-conscious for having said it at all.

Pre-child, thinking about how my body looked or wondering if my partner was getting bored would have stopped me from patiently accepting the long and peculiar process of my own pleasure unfolding. Now I understood how taking care of someone feels good to the person doing it. I felt too that I deserved it. I'd put in three years, and if someone now wanted to put three hours into me, I'd be woman enough to take it.

And then, finally, I'd absorbed my fill, and I began to return his favors. I was Shiva, and with my four arms, I showered the pompadoured bass player with a blizzard of bliss, until a yellow light shone out of *him*. I gave him a tit-fuck while jerking and blowing him and scooting up so that his knee could give me an orgasm all at the same time. I even got my hair into the act, swinging it back and forth so that the tips brushed against his scrotum. At one point I remember rubbing my shoulder against the bottom half of that mile-long rod while the top half stayed securely in my mouth. He was worth risking a dislocated shoulder, or even tongue. "Well, Doctor," I'd stutter in the emergency room, "it was like this...."

As dawn peered in at us from behind a drawn shade, I performed a pedicure on the feet of this man's soul—the $150 pedicure, the one that goes all the way up your leg, with sea salt and mud and hot wax and warm towels and nail polish that won't chip for weeks. I moistened him with tears and dried him off with gentle breath. I did it with all the enthusiasm of a teenager sneaking around with a cute person on the back stairs, except with the added tricks of a grown woman. And then I said I had to go.

My bass-playing date wanted to do it *again,* but I had to get back to my kid. Should I tell my date about my son, I wondered? Did I want to see him again? What could this fellow and I have in common—he with his unfettered rock'n'roll life, performing songs about leather straps and cool cars; me struggling to smile as Barney sings out at me day after day about tying my shoes and touching my toes.

"There's always that nagging question," is how my single mom friend Bernie describes it. "When do you tell him that you have a kid? You don't want to be deceptive, but you also don't want to blurt it out before you've even taken a bite of food. Will he suddenly picture you as having a stretched vagina, being frazzled? I always end up confessing after the third Chardonnay."

I saw something so horrifying on a dating show once. The guy said he didn't want his date because he knew she had a kid—she was wearing a halter-top, and he said he saw faint stretch marks (I couldn't see any). That guy made the biggest sex mistake of his sex life. There's no lover alive like a sneaking single mom lover. Pent-up by her caring, cloistered life, when she goes out, she *goes out.* She gets it in, gets it on, and gets out (has to get back home). Just like a man. Which is really what all men want—another man, but with a vagina. (Yes, I said *all* men. Don't start arguing with me. This is *my* essay, and if it's efficient for me to generalize, generalize I will!)

I ended up saying nothing about my son that night/morning to my new swain, and I saw him twice more over the next several weeks, under the same, glorious circumstances. And then, on our fourth scheduled date, both my parents got sick, so they couldn't watch my son. I brought him to New York, arranging to leave him for a couple of hours with Kate, who had originally set me up with the Pompadoured God.

P.G. said he'd swing by our mutual friend's place to pick me up between nine and ten. I wanted my son to be asleep in the guest room when P.G. arrived so that the concept of his little but huge existence, which had since come up, would remain one-dimensional. My son had other plans. His bedtime of eight o'clock came and went. He threw his book about a smiling train to the floor. Kate tried. She read about three pages of Klaus Kinski's autobiography to my boy, which for some reason had a stimulating effect on him. It was now nine o'clock and I understood that my son was never going to sleep again. I prayed that P.G. would be operating on New York time, which means arriving three to six hours late. But it seems P.G. was operating on can't-wait-to-have-great-sex time, and at exactly 9:30, the buzzer rang.

P.G. sat down with a beer, leaning back on the rickety kitchen chair and not looking at all as disturbed and nervous as I felt. My son shot out from the bedroom, chasing Kate's dogs all around and through P.G.'s legs. "Hi," my sex god and my son said to each other. My son demonstrated the breakdance moves that Kate had just taught him, made jokes about bodily functions, and talked really fast about monsters and space travel—just generally was a boy—while we watched and waited. P.G. helped him work out the problem of not being able to afford an engine for the rocket ship he wanted to build: Use a window fan. Finally, at midnight, my son passed out on the floor, an exhausted dog wrapped in his fat little boy arms. P.G. and I tiptoed out.

We had never much talked before. Now we did. I found out that besides playing onstage for screaming fans (well, okay, this was New York . . . for glaring, cross-armed fans), P.G. also bussed dirty dishes. He was Italian and grew up in Brooklyn but had spent some time in Philadelphia. I talked about how I had to live within twenty minutes of a beach or else I got really mean. I learned that his favorite color was orange and black together; he learned that I don't have a favorite color and that I just don't get how anyone could have one. Discovering these things about him, and letting him see my son and vice versa, made him human to me, and once someone's human, they're no longer a god—well, not the kind of god you check out of the library of pleasure and return. They're no longer your rescue party. I had to think about his feelings, and I imagine the fact that I might have some feelings, too, outside the bedroom, occurred to him for the first time. We now had to consider Where This Was Going. Always before, we were simply There already. Now, we had to think of what my son would need out of Us, and there's just no place for that question in a virtual stranger's bedroom. The question hovered between us, hogging up all the space formerly occupied by that magnificent, long, hot, hard, vibrating, muscular COCK waving about. The cock felt guilty strutting across the bed, with the Question there. It hid inside me and did the normal penis things, cried its salty tears, and then it deflated and put some underwear on.

Single moms may be the best people in the world to have a little affair with, but for love, they are the most complicated. By mutual consent, P.G. and I never saw each other again. But I am grateful to him to this day. He got me back into the life thing. He reminded me that I can take as well as give. He reminded me that there's really stuff worth taking out there! And I wish I knew the name of that instructional video, so I could tell you now, and you could run out and buy it for everyone you know for Christmas, because boy, is it the gift that gives.

ardor

and

ache

everything i need to know about romance i learned from jane austen

(i just wish i'd taken her advice sooner)

ᗢ darcy cosper

Throughout my twenties (an epoch that, a few years back and with tremendous relief, I put behind me), I led the disastrous dating life that most young women do. I was very young, very naïve, of moderate looks and means, well versed in Madonna and Camille Paglia, and living in a large, cosmopolitan city. In short, I was a recipe for the very disaster that I became.

Like many young women, so benightedly eager was I for a beau that my selection process was, I confess, rather compromised. For a time, to all appearances, my sole prerequisite for a mate was that he be bipedal and, if at all possible, bipolar. During more discriminating periods, I demanded men with great ambitions, great good looks, and egos to match. Above all, I was attracted to men who wanted absolutely nothing to do with me, and I pursued them with brio; in a pinch I would settle for a man who was merely ambivalent and set about to bring him around, perfectly convinced that my persistence would eventually triumph.

I remained, strangely, single. I grew baffled and bitter. Though morally certain that the real fault lay with those mad, bad, intimacy-averse boys, I had a stray suspicion that there was, perhaps, some minor flaw in my philosophy, some false step in my approach, an elusive *sagesse* that might lead me to love—but where and how would I discover it? Whither enlightenment?

Of course, all along and unbeknownst to me, I was already in possession of the wisdom of the ages—in the ouevre of Ms. Jane Austen.

More than two centuries before Helen Gurley Brown and Gloria Steinem, before *The Rules* and Girl Power, before Carrie Bradshaw and *Buffy the Vampire Slayer*, Austen knew everything there was to know about social machinations, gender politics, and the Byzantine complexities of romantic intrigue—and she wrote about them with perspicacity and preternatural insight. Today, she is often shrugged off as a mere romance writer, an author of drawing-room dramas and cunning little novels of manners (and perhaps, for the very woman who simultaneously invented and subverted the literary genre now identified in those most denigrating of terms— "Chick Lit"—to be thus misapprehended and undervalued is ironically appropriate). But readers who scratch the gleaming Masterpiece Theater–miniseries surface with which Austen's works have been shellacked will discover—in addition to the Wildean wit and Shakespearean scope—a profound intelligence and ferocious pragmatism, in particular with regard to the eternal warring and wooing of the sexes.

It was during my heady dating heydey that I first read (and then reread, and read again) *Pride and Prejudice* and *Sense and Sensibility*, *Emma* and *Persuasion*, *Mansfield Park* and *Northanger Abbey*. Had I only been paying closer attention, I might have caught on to the fact that each of these books is a sociopsychological Baedeker's Guide, and Austen a consummate sherpa of courtship; I might have taken the stealthy, superb advice her novels contain and thereby been spared a good deal of humiliation and heartache.

Today, having at long last caught on, and gotten with Jane's program, I find that the timeless principles that served her early nineteenth-century heroines will serve us twenty-first-century women equally well. And so, forthwith, The Rules According to Austen—so that you, gentle reader, might benefit from wisdom others overlooked and remain steady where others have stumbled.

I. Don't Make the Quest for a Man Your Priority

> It is a truth universally acknowledged, that a single man in possession of a good fortune must be in want of a wife.
>
> —*Pride and Prejudice*

Austen's heroines are, famously, headed for marriage, if not actually in pursuit of it—and this, of course, is part of her joke. In that oft-cited opening line of *Pride and Prejudice*, one can detect Austen's sly mockery of the inverse assumption: that an unmarried woman must be in want of a single man of good fortune. Sure, these novels *seem* preoccupied with romantic liaisons and "suitable matches," but Austen's thinly veiled sarcasm and suspiciously tidy endings suggest, to me, that the author believed that matrimony, far from being a woman's greatest achievement, was merely the only course open to her at that moment in history.

Austen reserves some of her most outrageous satires and savage judgments for women who are overinvested in the great husband hunt. The man-mad females who populate her novels—whether the giddily infatuated girl; the calculating flirt who sets out to marry a fortune; or the grasping matron who manipulates and maneuvers her daughters into contact with eligible bachelors—are represented as ugly and utterly contemptible. Such women, Austen instructs us, are to be disdained and pitied not so much for the vulgarity of their behavior (though there's plenty of it to disdain) as for the infinitely more unattractive lack of self-respect and self-reliance that such behavior reveals—and reinforces.

I have personally served hard time as this sort of single-minded single girl (see above), and I don't recommend it. It's counterproductive—few and far between are the men who find a desperate woman desirable—and ultimately quite boring. I strongly suggest, and I'm quite sure Austen would back me up on this, that you cultivate a hobby instead.

2. Don't Be Dazzled by Charm and Good Looks

> [The ladies] were worth pleasing, and were ready to be
> pleased; and he began with no object but of making
> them like him. He did not want them to die of love; but
> with sense and temper which ought to have made him
> judge and feel better, he allowed himself great latitude
> on such points.
>
> —*Mansfield Park*

Have you ever fallen in love (or into bed) with a very handsome man and awakened to regret it? Or been swept off your feet by a very charismatic man who turned out to be a cad? Or infatuated with a man who was unusually well spoken, well dressed, well behaved, well educated—only to discover that his character was not as attractive as his characteristics?

I, for one, am mightily guilty. For years, I was in the habit of swooning for austere blondes with impeccable résumés, witty redheads with large vocabularies, broody brunets with epic social skills and cute sports cars. And with the objects of my affection chosen according to such merits, I didn't experience much felicity on the relationship front, as well you might imagine. Many were the glaring defects and warning signs I overlooked in exchange for scimitar-like cheekbones and sexual prowess—and many the commitment issues, overinflated egos, and not-quite-ex–girlfriends that I might have taken note of earlier had I not been blinded by ravishing smiles and rippling abs.

Austen understands. She's an expert on bad men who look good; irresistible louts figure prominently in every one of her novels. Debonair and passionate men, amiable and agreeable men, noble-browed and broad-shouldered and well-bred men turn out to be wayward nephews who defile and desert innocent girls, adoptive sons with scandalous secrets and gambling habits, impoverished cousins with designs on dowries—or desirable bachelors who are simply otherwise engaged.

Austen recognizes the ubiquity and power of such men, and she sympathizes with the women who respond to their charms; even her smartest heroines are not immune. But while she forgives us for being taken in, Austen makes it perfectly clear that the fault lies not wholly, or even primarily, with the rakes and cads. These potentially dangerous and eminently avoidable follies are most commonly the result of— *nota bene*, gentle reader—our own impetuosity and vanity.

Which leads us to Austenian Rule Number 3.

3. Don't Let Your Heart— or Your Ego—Run Away with You

I have frequently detected myself in such kind of mistakes, in a total misapprehension of character ... and I can hardly tell why, or in what the deception originated. Sometimes one is guided by what [people] say of themselves, and very frequently by what others say of them, without giving oneself time to deliberate and judge.

—*Sense and Sensibility*

In Austen's moral universe, the sin of haste is the wellspring of more problems than almost any other sin is. Haste, she counsels, will lead us to misjudge personalities, to mistake intentions, to approve and attach ourselves to those we should shun, to condemn and censure where we should admire and applaud.

Numerous are the Austenian characters who fail to practice prudence, and they suffer for it—and numerous the modern girls who follow in their footsteps. More than once, in my callow youth (and, I'm sorry to say, more recently), I met with some mysterious stranger who, in addition to being apparently perfect, also had the good sense to be smitten with me. In every case, he was neither the one nor the other—but I had already swooned and surrendered and laid my heart at his feet, within handy trampling distance, before I found that out.

Though this counsel sounds obvious, it bears repeating: Have a few more dates with that perfect man before you decide he's your Mr. Knightley in shining armor.

4. Don't Overlook the Underdog, or the Man under Your Nose

> How to understand it all! The blunders, the blindness of her own head and heart! How long had [he] been so dear to her, as every feeling declared him now to be? When had his influence, such influence, begun?
>
> —*Emma*

One danger of not abiding by Rule Number 3 is that you are far more likely to violate Number 4, which is very nearly paramount among those Austen lays out for us.

The right men are hard to find, Austen suggests, only because we are looking in the wrong places for the wrong things. A true hero must be a true gentleman, and it isn't as simple as you might think to spot one, identifiable as they are by virtues made visible only over time: integrity, honesty, honor, courage, compassion, fortitude. It is a quintessential Austenian pickle that such qualities are overlooked—and opportunies for true love therby nearly lost forever!—because certain young ladies have not yet developed the ability to recognize and prize such merits as they should.

A few years ago, I began at long last to absorb the principles on which this particular Austenian tenet is founded. The list of attributes I required in a potential beau was revised to include just three qualities: he must be happy, courteous, and kind.

Soon after, I met just such a man. He was not one of the outgoing, ambitious, arrogant men for whom I had always fallen but a quiet, mild, modest man; not a social mover and shaker, nor a captain of industry, but a man who genuinely enjoyed his life and work and whose great ambition was not international fame or a seven-figure salary but a useful, peaceful existence.

Early in our relationship, I foolishly thought I might be making a sacrifice, exchanging my dream of a dashing romantic hero for the possibility of simple romantic happiness. But it soon became apparent that this good and gentle man was also wittier than the Ph.D.s I had dated; more sensitive than the poets (and a great deal less self-involved); his powers of observation and insight greater than those of the professional intellectuals for whom I had pined—in short, the smartest, the strongest, the best man of my acquaintance. He was—and is—a man of great good character, as Austen would say; he is a man who resembles those with whom her heroines at last achieve conjugal bliss; he is a hero of whom, I believe, she would approve.

However:

5. Don't Expect a Relationship to Make You a Happy Woman

I could never be so happy as you. Till I have your disposition, your goodness, I never can have your happiness.

—*Pride and Prejudice*

Make no mistake. Austen is not a romantic.

Don't be fooled by those love-conquers-all grand finales; her ostensible happy endings—sometimes little more than codas—tie things up too perfectly to be anything but parodies, or at best mild mockeries. When, for example, an impediment to marriage appears a mere page from the end of *Northanger Abbey*, Austen pokes fun at the characters, the readers, herself, and the literary and social conventions involved: "The anxiety . . . can hardly extend, I fear, to the bosom of my readers, who will see in the tell-tale compression of the pages before them, that we are all hastening together toward perfect felicity." And in his dazzling essay on *Sense and Sensibility*, critic David Gates points out that the happily-ever-after ending that sends the darling Dashwood sisters off into the English sunset with their respective husbands is composed of double and triple negatives; it's unlikely, he suggests, "that a writer so alive to words could have been deaf to the tone of [such] a sentence . . . or oblivious to its implicit meaning: that even people who love each other had better not get too close."

Austen makes it very clear to us that love and marriage have no inherent transformative or ameliorative powers. Her portraits of marriages that have matured beyond newlywed stage range from uninspiring to downright hellish. Even the notable exceptions to this rule further illustrate Austen's belief that no one is made happy by marriage in and of itself. Like many of us, I was indoctrinated early into the cult of the happy ending, its promise dangled temptingly in every bedtime story, every film and television ad and billboard: The right man would make me whole, the right relationship would make me content, and when these came to me, I'd live happily ever after, romantically blissful and personally fulfilled.

Imagine my surprise. I have, to the extent that it's possible and for as long as it lasts, achieved something like the romantic ideal—and still I find myself breathtakingly capable of snits and sloth and self-loathing, anxiety and ennui, and the general malaise that was supposed to be permanently eradicated by marriage (or, in my case, its modern equivalent, committed cohabitation).

I had to find true love before I could truly understand Austen's most important, and most radical, point: The happiness that she suggests may be in store for her heroines and their suitors, and for her readers, will arise not from love alone. Rather, it will come from inner resources and reasonable expectations; it is not passions of heart but qualities of mind that are the foundation of personal satisfaction, conjugal and otherwise.

In Austen's world—and in ours—couples achieve together only as much happiness as each is capable of attaining individually. Each of us is responsible, she insists, for our own happiness.

What could be less romantic than that—and what could be more true?

cut and shave

∽ laurie notaro

A s soon as he looked at me with that wicked little glint in his eye, I knew the drought was almost over.

It had been a long, dry season.

If my sex life was a farm, Willie Nelson and John Cougar Mellencamp would have been staging benefit concerts for it, because apparently, I couldn't even grow mud. There I was, right smack in the middle of my juicy, barely ripe twenties, when opportunities are typically bountiful and I should have had an after-dark social calendar akin to a sailor on leave. Instead, for months I was essentially living the life of a Brontë sister, trudging home to my empty abode after an evening out, peeling open a Lean Cuisine and letting infomercials keep me company until my Tylenol PMs called it a night.

Now, as far as I could tell, the reasons for the lack of prospects on my dating horizon were somewhat of a mystery: Although it was a given that my mug, complete with a really-only-visible-under-direct-sunlight Italian girl mustache, would never be crowned one of *People* magazine's 50 Most Beautiful, my metabolism hadn't yet slowed down to that of a speed bump, so physically speaking, I was in okay shape. The omitted tooth that had been pulled because I hadn't been able to afford a crown was thankfully a molar, and its absence could not be detected without a Maglite and a tongue depressor. And, on more than one occasion, a drunk man had told me that I had nice eyes, although in each instance it was the same drunk guy and his fly was down both times, so honestly speaking, it was rather hard to trust his judgment. But if you average out the mustache and the missing tooth with my size-ten ass and the nice eyes, well, things could have been worse.

But business, nevertheless, was slow. It just seemed as if every potential qualified dating candidate in my social circle had either hooked up, paired off, or just been admitted to rehab or a correctional facility. The ones that were left over were left over with good reason, unless I simply could no longer repress my hankering for the fellow that had the sole talent of being able to rip the cap off a beer bottle with his teeth or the guy that obviously couldn't manage the complex workings of the zipper on the front of his pants.

But now, after what had seemed like an abnormally long stretch that was becoming so intolerable it almost had me entertaining an offer from the "Nice Eyes, Fly Down" fellow, I believed the dry spell was coming to an end. I was at an after-hours party when I spotted a charming-looking gentleman on the far side of the room. I immediately recognized him as a guy I had had a secret little crush on and with whom I had engaged in slight mutual flirtation from time to time, although I had promptly forgotten about him after he'd moved to San Francisco to join a band a year earlier.

By the looks of it, he was back, and I decided to spring into action. Who knew if he was back for good, or maybe a short weekend visit? I was, however, acutely aware that I was taking a chance by attempting to talk to my object of desire, firstly because I had had a bit to drink thus far in the evening, but additionally, because of other dilemmas as well. It seemed as if every time I'd made an attempt to talk to this particular fellow, the fickle fist of fate had stepped in and interjected tragedy in the place of a condom.

The first time it had happened, I had finagled my way onto a bar stool next to his at the regular watering hole, and quickly, polite conversation turned to an obvious attraction. With a couple of drinks under my belt, my confidence blossomed into that of a size six, and I thoroughly believed that I was witty and beguiling and that sucking in my paunch was actually working. Sparks were definitely shooting back and forth, and a wink from my friend Sara, the bartender, confirmed this.

It seemed like magic, and if it wasn't for the insistent tugging of my bladder, I could have stayed on that stool all night.

But I didn't.

Instead, I'd slid off the stool, said I'd be right back, and then turned to head for the ladies' room just as Stacey, the waitress, was heading toward the kitchen carrying a tray full of gnawed, suckled, and ravaged buffalo wing remnants.

It was over in an instant, the witnesses said, and then there I was, laid out on my back on the floor as if I was getting prepped for childbirth, a lump the size of a neglected tumor quickly forming on my forehead, a ringing in my ears from being head-butted by restaurant china, and my paunch no longer sucked in.

I imagine it was a gruesome spectacle, but at the time, I was too concerned with the fact that I could only see out of one eye. I briefly thought that a chicken leg shard had skewered my cornea until Sara lifted a large, flappy canvas of chicken skin off the left side of my face as Stacey tried to wipe the wing sauce from my nose.

The boy I had been trying to light a love fire with simply looked on for a moment, chugged the last of his beer, and then vanished.

But the spark was rekindled when I saw him a couple of weekends later at the same bar. I tried to laugh off the buffalo wing incident, and I think he was trying to be kind when he mentioned that my forehead wound was healing nicely.

After that bumpy start, things became a little smoother. As I relaxed a bit, I pulled out a cigarette and realized I was out of matches. I believe he saw this as an opportunity to be smooth himself, and he presented a vintage, brushed-chrome Zippo lighter with three letters etched across the bottom of it.

"It was my grandfather's," he said, pointing to the mono-gram as he beamed proudly. "He had it with him all during World War II. But his doctor made him quit smoking, so he gave it to me. And you're the first one I get to light it for."

"Wow, that's really nice," I said, duly impressed as I put the cigarette in my mouth.

All I really remember after that was a big flash of light, the gasps of people around me, and the smell of something burning, which turned out to be my eyebrow. Right down to the skin, including some of it.

"I am so sorry," he said repeatedly, holding my cocktail to my head as a cold compress. "I guess Grandpa liked a really big flame, he has glaucoma."

I chugged the rest of my cold compress and left in search of painkillers and a skin graft.

In time, my eyebrow slowly regenerated, the welt on my head eventually vanished, and I found myself at the aforementioned party, standing across the room from my secret crush, the chicken-wing Zippo guy. I had one more chance to ignite a burning bonfire of desire—or at least one night of fun—as long as I wasn't impaled, gored, or mortally maimed before we got to the good part.

Fully aware that I should probably embark on this mission in nothing less than a HAZMAT suit, I decided to take my chances and worked my way through the crowd to where my secret crush stood, next to a guy in a tank top who'd just announced: "Watch me make bull's-eye!" and was now orally wrestling with a bottle of Bud Light. The tank top guy puffed out his chest like a rooster, puckered, and shot the cap from his mouth in the direction of a dartboard, where it predictably hit the bull's-eye and lodged itself.

"*Whooooo!*" he shouted to a petite round of applause.

I caught my secret crush rolling his eyes and decided to pounce on the opportunity.

"What a talent," I mentioned, nodding toward the tank top guy. "With your lighter and the blowhole of that guy's mouth, you guys could start your own circus."

My crush chuckled and smiled.

He had moved back to town a couple of weeks ago, he explained. Things just hadn't worked out in San Francisco.

"Oh, that's good," I replied. "Where are you living?"

"Here, actually," he told me. "This is my apartment."

"Oh, that's very good," I nodded with a very big smile. "You throw a very noisy party."

"We should go somewhere and talk," he offered. "I think we have a lot to catch up on. It's quieter . . . back there. Is that okay?"

"Sure," I agreed and followed him through the crowd and down the hallway.

"This is it," he said, opening the door to his bedroom. Then he stopped to look at me. "Hey, eyebrow looks good."

"Why, thank you," I responded. "It's funny how nature has its own way of clearing out the brush."

He laughed, but all of a sudden, just in that instant, my blood ran cold. I suddenly realized that I hadn't expected this. I hadn't prepared for this. For a really long time, the only available guys were the ones out there in the living room, cheering at a bottle cap on a dartboard.

In other words, the brush had not been cleared in several significant areas. And I mean *significant areas.* The garden, so to speak, had not been tended because I hadn't had any idea that company *might be coming over*! And, frankly speaking, a mustache was just the beginning of the gifts my Italian heritage had bestowed upon me. I mean, there was no way that a simple "lights out" trick was going to cover up what I had going on in an assortment of different places! Never mind the visuals, just the touch sensation alone would be more than enough for him to question if he was rolling in the sack with a Yeti, and to come to the conclusion that it was a male Yeti at that.

"Can I use your bathroom?" I said quickly.

"Yeah, it's right there," he said, pointing to a door directly adjacent to his.

"I'll be back in a minute," I said as I smiled, trying not to let the panic seep through.

I shut the door to the bathroom and stood there. What should I do? What was I going to do? *Shit!* I screamed inside my head. *Shit, shit, shit!* I dug through my purse for something, anything, although I don't know what I hoped to find—a roll of Scotch tape in a primitive version of a bikini wax, or a Swiss Army Knife to cut each hair one by one with a little, tiny inch-long scissors? I came up empty-handed, just as I suspected I would, and so I really had no choice. Really. There was no choice to be had. What choice was there?

I began quietly going through the drawers under the sink and the medicine cabinet, digging past the Mennen, shuffling through the Tinactin, peering over the Rogaine, and then finally, I hit gold.

One single, solitary (and used) Bic razor.

Thank God.

Now, I turned on the faucet and tried to be very economical about my maneuvers, but to tell the truth, catching up on six months' worth of maintenance with a rusty, used Bic and a silly little bathroom sink simply wasn't going to cut it. Literally. At one point I thought the only thing that could possibly save me was a weed whacker. There were vital regions that I needed access to that I couldn't reach, and that would very likely require the rinsing capacity of a hose. A little splash here and there was hardly inadequate; it was impossible.

Then I heard a knock at the door. "Are you okay?" my secret crush asked. "Are you brushing your teeth or something?"

"No, no," I stuttered, fumbling for an answer. I couldn't very well just blurt out, "I'm just using you or your roommate's nasty old Bic to tame my wild parts because I'm a dirty girl and don't keep up with these things unless it's absolutely necessary," so I said, "Someone spilled a beer on me and I'm trying to wash it off."

"Oh," I heard from the other side of the door. "Okay."

When I was sure I heard him go back into his room, I went back to work, only to realize that everything I had shorn was now sticking to me, all over, just like when you get a haircut, only I had no pants on. I looked like an animal with mange.

What the hell, I thought as I looked at the shower, I've come too far to turn back and abandon the mission altogether. I've just come too far. I stepped into the tub and turned the water on.

The shower was a miracle. I rinsed, groomed, trimmed, and, as an extra bonus, was even able to freshen up a bit with a little chunk of Irish Spring I found.

"Hey," I heard from the other side of the door. "Are you . . . taking a *bath*?"

"No," I called from the shower. "The beer stain was bigger than I thought. I think I might have to soak it."

"Do you need some laundry soap?" he asked.

"Yes! That would be wonderful," I exclaimed, figuring that would give me enough time to get out, dry off, and get dressed.

And it was. When I got out of that shower, I felt ten, no, *fif-teen* pounds lighter. I had depleted the forest so successfully that I was almost cold. The new, molted me got dressed and came out of the bathroom only to find an empty bedroom.

Hmmm, I thought as I looked around. Surely that was enough time to find soap. I sat on the bed at the precise time I heard a sharp yell over and above the din of the party. The whole apartment became very quiet.

It was foolish of me not to guess, but when I got to the living room, I just nodded.

Everyone was standing still, except for the guy in the tank top, who was waving his hands and shouting over and over, "Dude, I said bull's-eye! I said bull's-eye, dude!"

Because there, next to the tipped and leaking bottle of My-T-Fine laundry detergent, sat my secret crush with one hand covering one eye and the other hand grasping a bottle cap.

girl times two minus one

~~ rachel mattson

G o ahead and fall in love with me. I mean that as a warning. Go ahead and shut the door, turn on the light, put your cheek against the wall. Say hello. *I'm in the kitchen,* I'll tell you, *with my head in the freezer.* Give me a minute to thaw my face out, and I'll come over to poke your belly. *Hi gorgeous.* But I won't fall in love back. I'm through with that.

Three years ago I sat on the edge of a twin bed in a hotel room above Forty-third Street and put on my shoes. Big clunky black ones. And tied the laces. A girl was dressing in the bathroom, a girl smelling of frankincense and tea tree oil, blow-drying her hair, buttoning her uniform, singing to me in Spanish. I felt hydroelectric. Let me just find my glasses, stand up straight, pick up my bag, I thought. Jeez, pull your shit together.

I don't think about girls much these days, except as abstractions, except as memories or people to meet for coffee. Not possibilities, not reasons to breathe. I go home at night and turn on a lamp and water the plant and clean off the countertop. It suits me fine.

My parents are at the point where they're trying to get me to go to lesbian singles' night at their synagogue. I picture the whole thing as a mess of long brown hair, corduroy, light-colored jeans from the Gap, and conversations about where to find the cleanest public restrooms on the Upper West Side. What happened to the days when my parents were too homophobic to even know about lesbian singles' nights?

The frankincense girl, Elsa, took me to Vieques one time, and we stretched out naked on the rice-colored sand, then oiled our hair and tough-girled our way through town in a rented red Jeep. There was only one ATM on the island, and for some reason we forgot to bring cash, so we stood in line on the sidewalk, sun like a lemon, the sky a pitcher of warm water, dizzy with brightness, trying to do mathematical calculations. One night we got into a fight over nothing and she stormed off to an outdoor bar, where she bought a painting off the wall and made the bartender tell her about local politics. When she came back I was asleep. She was so drunk that she puked into the wicker wastebasket next to our bed. Stripping off the last of her clothes, she asked me to hold her. I held her.

Q: What does a queer girl bring on the second date? A: A U-Haul.

When we visited her grandma's house in Rio Piedras, we stayed in her sister's room, all pink and bunk beds and paper cutouts of Justin Timberlake. She let her *abuela* think I was just a drinking buddy of hers. She was known for her drinking buddies. I got on the top bunk and she got on the bottom bunk and switched off the lights. On the other side of the door I could hear Abuela ambling in her nightgown from bathroom back to bedroom, and then I could hear her close the door. "Whatcha doing up there?" Elsa whispered, and I could hear her smiling. I jungle-gymed down to her bunk. She licked my neck. "Cover my face with a pillow so no one will hear," she said. "You're insane," I said. Her *abuela* was a Seventh-day Adventist, and I really didn't want to deal with what that meant. The walls were particleboard thin. "Tocala," she begged, just touch her.

At some point I decided it was too hard to be a zeppelin, filled to bursting and floating like a carnival thrill across the sky. Sometimes I want to be a shirt, a pedestrian just crossing the street. Sometimes I am happy to be shapeless. If you're a zeppelin, even just lying in bed holding hands with someone can break your heart and send you to the bathroom to look at your hands, trying to come down, trying not to explode from feeling.

One time I brought her to my cousin's birthday party. It was a fancy affair at my aunt and uncle's Central Park West apartment, just exactly the kind of thing I try to avoid. The kind of event where you have to stand around being nice to people; you have to discuss the plotlines of popular movies and the resilience of the stock market. My uncle greeted us at the door and took our coats. "You're from Puerto Rico?" he said to her. "I knew this guy from Puerto Rico once." He was trying to be nice. In the bathroom, later, she stared out the window. From that bathroom window, as it happens, you can see the midsection of the park, all lit up, and people, like animals, moving around between the trees. You can see glowing buildings lined up all along Fifth Avenue across the way. That bathroom's like a gold-plated Frank Sinatra song. New York, New York: It's a wonderful town. "I feel weird," she said. "I never even knew anyone lived like this."

It's hard to know when you're acting out a prearranged narrative and when you're just trying to love a girl.

Did you ever see that movie *White Palace*, starring James Spader and Susan Sarandon? He's a rich, professional Jew and she's a working-class goyish waitress. They meet and he's all nervous and *what did you say to me?* and she's flirty and smoking a cigarette, and eventually they have this impulsive, scorching sex. But then she goes home with him for Thanksgiving and that's it: Somebody in James Spader's family says something liberal but offensive about the stupidity of blue-collar voters and then Susan Sarandon gets up and tells them all off. Later she tries to break up with James Spader and he's like, *Wait, no I love you*, and she's like, *Man this is never going to work*, and he's like, *Why not, come on*. When me and Elsa split I rented that movie again and cried the whole time.

Then I adopted a cat.

One imagines that things will get easier to understand as time passes; I'm starting to think it's the other way around.

It's strange to think, but actually I've only gone on four real dates in my life: once when I was visiting my brother in L.A.; once in Provincetown; once with Elsa; and once, by mistake. The girl in L.A. had been raised by Mormons. She took me to a restaurant on Melrose, the kind that has outdoor seating and those enormous heat lamps standing about everywhere like electric palm trees. I think I wanted to kiss her, just for the sheer novelty of being on a date and kissing someone, but both of us lost our nerve and then I never saw her again.

Elsa brought a suitcase to our first date. It was a midsized Travelpro with wheels. She'd bought it with her American Airlines employee discount a couple weeks earlier. I ran my hand over the black canvas along the front, unzipped a pocket, and said, "Yeah, nice," but I was thinking, Oh, fuck. I tried not to make a metaphor out of it. I reminded myself she had to fly to work in the morning.

Looking back now, it seems inevitable that things would go wrong. She owned several pairs of leather pants; I have a collection of sensible socks. When we met, I was in love with someone else. The last time she had been in love, she'd been married and living in a lighthouse. Years ago.

As for second dates, I don't think I've ever actually been on one. After that first night with Elsa, for instance, we just immediately started meeting up in my bed. She would show up at my apartment with her grin and her suitcase. Behind her, Brooklyn would be some fabulously wet green color, even in the pitch black of a winter night. Then she'd brush past me and we'd be horizontal in minutes. Once in a while she took a shower first. Sometimes I gave her a Coca-Cola.

I admit it: I was scared. Do you blame me?

Sex with her was the kind you wish for a long time after it ends. I can't remember the details anymore—it was unreal, I was out of my head—and so I lie in my bed with my hand on my own neck, wishing I could. I remember some things, like the time I got my fist inside her and she bucked and bucked and then fell asleep with her hand between my legs; I remember the time she kept her lips to my ear as she took me, the whole time telling a twisted story about two schoolgirls in their uncle's Trans Am. But there's no longer enough detail in my memory to get my hips moving against whatever toy I've dug out of my drawer.

I used to have a story I told about what has happened to me—the demented suburban childhood, the book-filled adolescence, the way my first love turned weightless and floated away, how loving a second time eroded me—but now this is gone, too. Fogged over like the metal mirror in my bathroom. Not being in love, I'm thinking, is like not knowing where the story begins and where it ends; first there was a girl, then she broke your heart, then you began to heal the brokenness. Then you waited for something else to happen.

Even the most unremarkable moments with Elsa seem to tell a story about race and class, possibility and hurt. I gave her a photograph of herself; she tore it up and dyed her hair. Someone played a Tito Puente song; she collapsed into tears.

One time a doctor surprised me by diagnosing me with a disease I had heard of but never imagined I was afflicted with. I still felt like crap, but suddenly, also, elated. *So that's what all that was about.* Until then, nothing was strung together; I'd simply been having a series of confusing episodes of bad feeling. Now all those hours of pain were a story. They were symptoms; I was sick. Ha! How great! When I was in love, the radio, the alarm, the bed, the academic conference, the Puerto Rican flag that hangs in her window, the time we fought until five in the morning, the time I lay on the floor and cried—they were part of the story. As soon as we were broken up, lying on the floor crying didn't have a narrative to attach to. It was just lying on the floor crying.

Is this the beginning, a prelude to something else? Or is this the place where the plot thickens and the narrator plants ideas that will sprout later? Maybe it's the ironic descent toward a foregone conclusion, this dwindling away toward endless hours of riding the subway and attending birthday parties? I'd just like to know; it would help.

She had these two Siamese cats that liked to sleep between her legs.

someone old, someone blue

ᘓ lynn harris

O n Saturday I reached fifty.

    I'm thirty-four years old, and single, and as of last Saturday night, I have attended fifty weddings.

Yes, fifty. Fifty weddings since I've been old enough to want one myself. At this point, shouldn't I at least get a watch, or a husband? Alas, Saturday's festivities at the Brooklyn Botanical Garden featured no Ally McInterlude wherein the MC interrupted the hora to present me with my walking, talking, ring-bearing Lifetime Achievement Award. Au contraire, in fact: the hot forestry Ph.D. who chatted me up all night vanished for Cambridge without so much as an "I'll email you."

Yes, fifty weddings. Just for the record, I include in my

tally one lesbian commitment ceremony, because (a) now *The New York Times* does, and (b) as the lesbian ritual was traditional in all other ways, I was forced to participate in the group line dance to the song "Hot! Hot! Hot!" No way am I not getting credit for that.

My wedding count would be fifty-one, actually, if I were to count my own wedding: a hilltop ceremony in 1980—with a processional by Journey and a ring from Spencer's Gifts—that united me with Kenny Spaziani. I mean, "Spaz" was cute, but he's not Jewish.

I have attended the weddings of friends, family friends, cousins, ex-boyfriends. I have gone with dates, sans dates, as a date. I have been to weddings in Vermont, Minnesota, and Louisiana; in Catalonia, Veracruz, and Tel Aviv. I went to my college roommate's wedding at the Brookings, South Dakota, Lions Club. I went to a wedding on Cape Cod where the bride and groom arrived and departed in a rowboat. I went to a summer wedding in Scarsdale in an open air-conditioned tent— yes, they were *cooling the outdoors*—with Porta Pottis that were nicer than my bathroom. I went to a foodies' wedding in Manhattan with six cheese tables, the night before I took a cholesterol test. I went to a power wedding at the Plaza where a toast to the couple included the words *inchoate* and *penumbra*. I went to a wedding in Maine where the bride wore wings. I went to a wedding in Napa in a glen of redwoods that was surely attended by gnomes. I went to a wedding in New Jersey featuring a vegetarian Indian dinner followed by a "Viennese Table." I went to a wedding in Maryland where I got hammered enough to sing "My Funny Valentine" with the band. I went to a wedding in Montana with my best friend as my date, and only later learned that the hot best man totally would have hooked up with me, but he thought we were lesbians. I went to a wedding in the Everglades where I got in trouble with my parents—always dignified when you are twenty-seven—for taking a late-night skinny-dip in the lake with the other younger guests. I was like, "MOOOOOM!!!" and she was like, "You didn't see the sign that said, NO SWIMMING: ALLIGATORS?"

I have been to the weddings of three ex-boyfriends, one of whom—my boyfriend emeritus, really—was the love of my life, at least when my life was twenty years long. At his wedding, I was like Jackie Kennedy, all fabulous and tragic in a great little dress. When I saw his parents hugging her instead, I felt just like George Bailey. "Esther! Bernie! Dontcha know me?"

There are now no longer enough singles to fill a "singles table." I am, at least, sometimes the bridesmaid. I recently served as Maid of Honorable Mention, as I like to call it (on darker days, Old Maid of Honor), at my cousin's wedding. I was beaming and helpful and made a killer toast and got very drunk and went straight from there to play ice hockey with my hair still up in a French twist under my helmet. I got two penalties for roughing.

The weekend before last, I attended the black-tie wedding of a fellow female comedian, thus reassured that funny women get married. I saw how the bride looked the groom right in the eyes, open and serene and sure. I flipped through mental slides of my exes, Forrest Gumping the two of us into the scene up at the altar—and thought, for each one, No. Which, actually, was faintly reassuring as well.

My date, meanwhile, wore his own tux: We tangoed, we jitterbugged, we canoodled. We kissed too, until he said, "You know, to kiss you more would be leading you on."

Taxi!

That was wedding number fifty. I cried all the way home in the taxi, not because my date had not proposed but because we live in a world where sometimes even the mensches have bad manners. I cried because I wanted a big party in honor of *me*; because I wanted to love someone enough to look at him like brides do; because I wanted to love someone enough to print it, on thick paper, in raised type you can touch. I cried because I wanted someone standing in my corner, watching my back, sharing the driving. I cried because I am so fucking sick of having to put down my parents as my "emergency contacts" when I fill out a form.

I also cried because we, single women of a certain age, are caught between a rock—that big honking rock we're all supposed to want—and a hard place. I have been told both to be more patient and to be less picky. Once I said to someone, "Sure, I'd like to get married," and she said, "Really? I didn't think of you that way!"

It's true. You can't win. If you say you're not married, people think, What's wrong with you? If you say you'd like to be married, people think, What's wrong with you? If you say you'd like to be married, people also think, Whoa, *tick tock!* If you say you don't care if you get married or not, people think, What's wrong with you? I have stopped saying much at all, other than perhaps a coy, jaunty "I'm dating"—leaving the other person's imagination to fill in "Benicio Del Toro."

As I sat on my stoop that night, after wedding number

fifty, I fished my teeny cell phone out of my teeny clutch and called my emergency contact.

"Mom?" I said.

"Oh, sweetie," she said. "You know, next time, if you don't feel like it, you don't have to go."

"Yes, I do," I said, quite sure.

Why so sure? First, because I love a party. Especially a black-tie party—where else do I get to wear the thousand-dollar shoes I got at the Jeffrey sale for ninety-nine dollars? Also because, duh, you're supposed to meet single men at weddings. (Number of dates I've gone on with guys I met at weddings: one. Number of weddings that person recently had in Geneva: one.) And also because it is worth it to me to hit wedding number 2,632 just to be able to send a reply card saying: *"Cal Ripken* will be delighted to attend."

But here's the main reason I will keep up my wedding streak no matter what. I may be the girl who cries in the cab on her way home, but I will *not* be the girl who doesn't go 'cause she can't deal. The day I can't raise a glass to my friends' joy, the day I let odds blot out hope, the day I don't get caught up in a really good hava nagila—*that* is the day I'll be truly alone.

That said, just for the record, I will officially no longer dance to "Hot! Hot! Hot!"

girl saves own life over worthless jerk

✐ heather white

It was New Year's Eve in Las Vegas. Things with Jake and me had not been going well all weekend, and his band was treating me with an uncharacteristic delicacy that gave me a queasy feeling in my stomach.

We were all there, in Vegas, because Jake's band had been invited to play at the preopening party of the brand-spankin'-new New York New York Hotel. This meant that the only people staying in the two-thousand–room hotel were the invited guests and a couple of bands with their managers, roadies, wives, and girlfriends—in that order. I was lowest on the totem pole, and it seemed that every time I would make an innocent suggestion, Jake would sneer at me.

"Let's play some blackjack, baby."

Sneer.

"We could go to our room and be the first to soil those crispy white sheets."

Sneer.

I was determined to make it work with Jake, but he hadn't touched me with actual "intent to fulfill" in months; so with that same determination, I made a point of pretending, just this weekend, not to care. I stayed in my room while the band set up for their show, and I dressed myself in vintage garter belts and a slithery cocktail dress from the fifties. Instead of joining the other wives and girlfriends for preshow drinks, I wandered through phony replicas of Greenwich Village and Park Avenue with my perfumed cleavage thrust up at a painted night sky. I sat on a velvet couch in the Deco supper clubs and had cocktails with a young Sinatra impersonator. I tried to ride the rooftop Coney Island roller coaster that shoots around the outside of the buildings, but they weren't taking passengers for a couple more days.

I took the elevator down from the roof to a random floor and walked the long, carpeted, empty corridors that reminded me of *The Shining*. The emptiness of the hotel matched the hollowness I felt, the heart-chilling, soul-numbing void, which was filling up, as my sadness often did, with desire. A door clicked open and an older couple rolled their room service cart out of their room, laughing all the way to the elevator. They never saw me lingering in the hall behind them. Their dining tray was stacked with silver service lids, two empty bottles of Veuve Clicquot, and various white plates smeared with remnants of dinner. Upon closer inspection, I noticed that one of the champagne bottles was only about a third of the way empty. I poured the ice water from the bucket into the various glasses left on the cart and took a huge, delicious slam of bubbly. With the half-full bottle in my right hand and the empty ice bucket in my left, I switched down the hall, quiet as earmuffs. At the end of a corridor was that little room with vending and ice machines. I slipped into the fluorescent-lit cubicle and put the champagne down on the floor. I was facing the ice machine, and the door was to my left. I imagine the security camera was behind me, above the soda machine, but I never turned around to check. I placed the bucket on the shelf and pressed the lever lightly so the ice came out slowly. As soon as the familiar rumble and gurgle of cubes started, I pressed my pelvis against the lip of the bucket and thrust forward about fifteen times in rapid succession until a hot ripple moved through my tensed thighs, up through my esophagus, and out of my throat in what felt like a rapturous vomit and sounded like a tiny whimper.

Midnight came and went while the band played, just as it had every year for the last three of my life with Jake. Afterward, the gang came back to the suite Jake and I were sharing, with its perfect white sheets and silk drapes, and there was the usual toasting and dancing. Jake sat in a corner and strummed his guitar, his delicate hands making me want to cry. I'd kept my red dress on, hoping he'd notice. Everyone else noticed. The wives and girlfriends told me how beautiful I looked, and the guys looked at my breasts, then away. I whispered to Jake that I was going to bed and he should tuck me in and say good-bye. He knew I was leaving the next morning, for work—inventory day at the store I managed. I found an available bed in a room next door and left the door open a crack, so he'd know where I was. But I must have fallen asleep waiting. The next morning I tip-toed over the sleeping bodies of the all-night party, the slack, drunk faces of my band family. Sentimental tears came to my eyes. I think I only missed the years I had wasted; I would not miss the people. I caught my flight, but I didn't go in to work. A management no-show on inventory day means no job the next day. It was a new year and I was fired.

I decided to start packing my things and have a talk with Jake when he got home in a week. On January 2, I was sorting through some old camping equipment in the garage, and something told me I had to open that Coleman stove. There it was—the heroin, the needles, the spoon. I knew everything now: where our money went, why our small, lazy dog needed such long walks, why every movie we rented lulled him to sleep, why he needed to lock the door when he studied music, why he grew more remote every day. I finally knew his mistress.

Then it was January 3, my birthday, and Jake didn't call. Early January 4 I called his room at the New York New York. A sweet girl answered his phone.

"Hi, honey, what's your name?" I asked tenderly, a cauldron of hatred boiling over inside my chest.

"June!" she answered cheerfully.

"Tell me, June? Is Jake around?" I inquired equally cheerfully.

"Just a minute, he just got out of the shower," she said.

A whole minute went by. And then June was back, whispering, "He's asleep."

"In the shower?"

"No," she cowered.

"In bed?" I said.

"Uh, I didn't see him."

"He just fucked you and now he's making you deal with me?"

"Uh-huh," June whimpered.

I felt sorry for this girl, but my anger far outweighed her plight. "June, honey, take a message and some advice: Tell him he can kiss his vintage record collection and his music equipment and me and his dog good-bye," I said in a trembling voice. "And you should slap him for making *you* break up with *me.*"

Click! I gathered up his coveted lifetime collection of records; all his beautiful guitars—including the one that had belonged to Les Paul; a stand-up bass; a mother-of-pearl–inlaid accordion from the thirties; and a trumpet, which he could not play, and I loaded them into the car with the bass neck sticking out the window.

The guys at Jake's favorite music store were used to women selling back their boyfriends' instruments. I had the receipts because I had bought them for him in the first place. I told them I would take as much as they could give that day. It was enough. At the "buy-sell-trade" record shop, the vinyl freaks gathered around my mother lode with their mouths agape, too busy pawing through Jake's collection to care about the crackhead in the back stealing hip-hop CDs. Jake never even called to save his precious collections.

By January 6, I was on a plane to the real New York, New York, with three bags, six oversized boxes, and the tiny dog (who'd never cared much for Jake) in tow. I had a girlfriend, Gina, who always told me, when I complained about my life, that I could come and stay with her.

Gina lived in a huge loft in Chinatown and worked as a stylist. In the movies, New York lofts are so magical and bright, so airy and sexy. White gauzy fabric hangs everywhere, and sculptures are part of the construction. This is not the true story of loft living. The true story, I found out, is that some creepy slumlord can't meet building codes for a factory so he lets the place out to artists and other ingenuous types who will live with no walls and little plumbing and hang heavy fabric everywhere to keep the heat in winter and the air-conditioning in the summer—and to keep soot, vermin, and carbon dioxide from flowing in through the crumbling mortar. God forbid one hangs white gauze!

Gina went to work all day while I froze to death in her loft. The small dog hated the cold. But he loved me endlessly—as long as I was around, he was grand, and that worked out fine because I had no place to go. I drank wine and tried to figure out what had happened to me.

I had always been a very sexual person. When I was five, my mother had had to pry me off the jet of a hot tub in front of guests at a party. I'd known what I'd been doing, but I hadn't thought any adult had figured out the sensual euphoria brought on by a hard stream of hot water; I'd thought I was safe, glued to that current like a monkey clinging to a tree branch. But now that I was grown up and the jets were no longer off-limits, I had lost my will to cling to them. Three years of Jake's methodical neglect and rejection had done something to that monkey-girl, plucked her from the jets and disengaged her from herself. If Jake could only smell the hatred I held for him. The man who'd fallen to his knees in an airport and begged me to marry him only one year ago now represented every rejection, every tiny cut, and every humiliation I had endured in my messy life. I would glue myself together again. I knew where to find the parts. Hadn't they all been there on New Year's Eve? Hadn't I recaptured myself that night in the red dress, pressed up against the rumbling ice machine, trembling with passion—and potential? I began to fantasize about my recovery.

Gina did prop and fashion styling for films and photo shoots, and I spent hours going through her stuff. She had tons of costumes, notions, and bolts of fabric and ribbon. I loved every yard of it, and so did the small dog. Gina told me to feel free, and I took this literally.

I wore nothing around the loft except pointy bras and garters with stockings. The uneven floors made heels hard to traipse around in, so I left them off. One night, when I heard Gina's key in the lock, I slipped on an authentic Japanese 1930s kimono and tied it loosely. Gina never knew that I carefully considered my outfits each day; she thought I was so sad that I couldn't get dressed. I felt the perverted delight of a flasher in his raincoat as we sat on the couch gossiping and giggling. That night she confided in me that she had a Slovenian lover with Muslim ties and a small penis. He treated her terribly in public and made a point of hitting on other women in front of her. She said the sex was incredible, mainly because of the filthy things he would say, and the best part was she didn't love him. I had my doubts about that.

The next morning, I got decked out in the sexiest outfit that thirty-degree weather would allow—very Julie-London-at-her-ski-cottage—and headed to the Garden of Eden sex shop, where I bought a giant, lifelike, flesh-colored cock with a purplish head and one tiny little clitorator.

Back at the loft, I stripped to my bra and panties and spent the next two and a half hours lacing up my legs, waist, arms, and neck with silk ropes and ribbons. Then I used various diameters of cord to bind the rest of my body, leaving my joints free to move. I was like a rag doll made from beautiful bits and pieces of pink, purple, baby blue, and red. Finally I laced my crotch, armpits, and breasts together with the most gorgeous black thin brocade rope. Only my head, hands, and feet were untouched by ties. All of these parts were starting to swell. The bedding was wet, and I was ready for Mister Flieshcock. I had named him that on my way home while he'd rested on tissue paper in an elegant plain brown sack.

The climax is so anticlimactic! I had been building up to this moment for three weeks, for years even? And what did it amount to but a few rhythmic pulses . . . and then a problem. I was in a bit of body shock. I could hardly feel my head or fingers anymore. Any person into bondage will tell you to have a good pair of scissors handy and never to do it by yourself. But don't you have to do it by yourself first to decide if you like it? I made it to the kitchen counter and slid a knife, blade side out, from my breastbone to my belly button so I could breathe. I imagined the humiliating headline: GIRL AUTO-ASPHYXIATES OVER WORTHLESS JERK.

But the ribbons fell away and the air poured into my lungs and the only humiliation I suffered was being walked in on by

Gina as I stood naked in her kitchen with withered ribbons, cords, and ropes around my ankles. Each binding had left its spiral imprint on my body, advertising what I had just done.

To her credit, Gina simply said, "Honey, I think you need a drink right about now."

"No shit," I said shyly.

She went to the closet and pulled out the kimono I loved to wear, holding it out to me. As I took it, I finally met her eyes, and we both burst out laughing.

"So, you're okay?" she asked.

"I'm okay," I said, belting the kimono tightly around my waist. "No, I'm better than okay. . . . I'm amazing."

waiting

~~ eliza minot

There are those years when it's you, all about you. Your apartment. Your job. Your boyfriend. Your time off. Your exercise. Your food. Your music. Your family. Your future. Where you live. What you do. What's going to happen to you? What are you waiting for? Are you waiting? What is it, really, that you want? You look for the inner you. Or is it the inner child? The child of the inner you? The inner child of the child within? You can't keep it straight. All you know is you, and that's just great. After all, you've been alone with yourself for your whole life anyway. Only now, you're a young adult. You can do anything.

What you do best is tiptoe around the edges of intimacy, avoiding yourself, trying to be yourself, having sex, leaving people, being left. Thinking, What will happen when I really grow up? Who will I really love? You rent your own apartment because you have your own job. You have your own vacations because you have your own job. You pay your own bills because you have your own job. You never save money. There's your family, back behind the trees in the distance. There are your friends, sometimes right there, sometimes not. There's your boyfriend (or not). Your cigarettes. Your Pilates class. . . . Sometimes everything feels empty, hard to face. What is wrong with you? You take long baths. You loll in the shower. Sometimes you go out dancing. Sometimes you try to go look at things, try to learn. Sometimes you sit still on your couch that you found on the street but is as good as new (you tell yourself, trying not to think of the many things that could have gone on atop it). You sit on the couch in your minuscule apartment. You look out at the airshaft and the potted plant you've put on the fire escape. You smoke cigarettes as though you are waiting. You live your life as though you're waiting. You wait for a phone call. From who, you're not exactly sure.

You get involved with guys for various reasons: who they remind you of, who they don't remind you of, what they make you think of yourself, what they don't make you think of yourself. Some are all-out jerks and losers (what's wrong with you, anyway?). Some are perfectly nice. And even though they seem to be the focus of your attention, they are beside the point. As for sex, the excitement of growing up, of being able to have sex at all, is no longer enough. Something happens to the landscape in front of you. What was once interesting-like-a-Third-World-country-where-you're-visiting-and-think-you-might-like-to-live—exotic, human, fascinating, easygoing—is suddenly intensely frustrating. You begin to notice that nothing works properly. The roads are pot-holed, with no signs—or signs misguiding you like a playful nightmare. The trash that gets burned, nightly, in the trenches alongside the road, fills the air with a toxic black smoke. The river is filthy. Women are washing in it. You suddenly have square, nerdy considerations for things like fire escapes, health care, prescriptions, signs on the highways, democracy, accurate maps, running water that you can drink. A decent shower. A good bed. These things would all make life better. These things would make sex better. It occurs to you: I am a grown woman now (growing, anyway, getting more grown). Calling yourself a woman, in all seriousness, gives you a squeamish, nervous feeling. There's a loneliness to it, but also pride, which you can taste in the back of your mouth. And Christ, all of that trying to read into people—guys—has been harder than you thought. You seem to have been hanging on to certain people for no good reason other than the fact that they make your issues apparent to yourself.

You think, I don't need it. I don't need their help anymore. And was anyone really helping me to begin with? But loneliness. . . . You meet someone new and for the first time, you wonder, Could I love this man? The answer? Obviously, no. When it happens, apparently, it isn't a question.

But better to be lonely, alone, than to be lonely with someone who distracts you from the feeling while actually making you lonelier. That took some time to get your head around. But still. It's lonely without love. No way around it.

You tell yourself you like being alone (you do, right?) and forge on, like one of those mice with minute eyes—a mole—

burrowing through dark tunnels of dirt, raising its head up from time to time: This way . . . ?

Or like in those movies about reproduction that show the sperm swimming fiercely, stupidly, toward their ultimate, unseen destination: bumping into walls, getting stuck in corners, some of them handicapped, jittering along their way, every one for himself. Pin the Tail on the Donkey, blindfolded, twirling.

And then you find him, or he finds you, comes swooping down, lifting you away—Tarzan taking Jane on the swinging vine. Or Jane grabbing on to him, the air rushing in her ears. Your exuberance! Your jungle call of victory! The world comes into focus—the male bolt fitting securely in its spot. Love is more than you even thought. Buds on the trees practically grow as you watch. Music is tactile. Tactile things are musical. From between your legs comes the two of you as one—blinking, self-contained, wary. Wondering why it's taken so long to get out.

I'm not thrilled to be saying that finding the guy is the happy ending to all of that waiting, but (for this bird) it is.

contributor biographies

GENEVIEVE FIELD is a senior editor at *Glamour*. She is the co-founder of the Web magazine *Nerve* (nerve.com), the editor of *Nerve: The New Nude,* and the coeditor of *Nerve: Literate Smut* and *Full Frontal Fiction*. She has also introduced several photography books and written and edited for MTV Books.

Authors

JULIANNA BAGGOTT is the author of three novels, *Girl Talk* (2001), *The Miss America Family* (2002), and *The Madam* (2003). She has also published a book of poems, *This Country of Mothers* (2001). Her work has appeared in dozens of publications, including *Best American Poetry 2000* and *Ms.*, and it was read on NPR's *Talk of the Nation*.

JENNIFER BAUMGARDNER (a New Yorker by way of Fargo) is the coauthor of *Manifesta: Young Women, Feminism, and the Future* (2000) and *Grassroots: A Field Guide to Feminist Activism* (2005), both written with her friend and writing partner, Amy Richards. She and Amy also co-own a speaker's bureau called Soapbox and have spoken at more than 150 colleges since *Manifesta* was published. She occasionally does things on her own, such as writing the book *Look Both Ways:*

Girls and Sex (2004), writing articles for magazines such as *Harper's, Elle,* and *The Nation,* and raising money for various do-gooder causes.

LILY BURANA is the author of *Strip City: A Stripper's Farewell Journey Across America* (2001). Her writing has appeared in *The New York Times, The Washington Post, New York* magazine, *GQ,* and many other publications. She lives in upstate New York.

LISA CARVER's father was a drug dealer, her mother a schoolteacher. She is an only child. Her favorite author is Dostoyevsky, and she used to be a prostitute. She started the bloody, naked, operatic performance troupe Suckdog in 1987; started publishing the fanzine *Rollerderby* in 1989; wrote the books *Rollerderby* (1996) and *Dancing Queen* (1996); became a columnist for *Nerve* in 1997; freelanced for *Hustler, Playboy, Newsweek, Index, Mademoiselle, The New York Times Magazine,* and many more. She has appeared on NPR, HBO, and MTV. In the middle of all this, Lisa was a single mother, so she has a lot of experience with hiding the kid from the men and the men from the kid.

DARCY COSPER is an ardent Victorian literature enthusiast. Her book reviews, essays, and short fiction have appeared in publications including BOOKFORUM, *The New York Times, The New York Journal News, Village Voice, GQ,* and *Nerve.* Her first novel, *Wedding Season,* was published in 2004. She lives happily in Los Angeles but consideres herself ambi-coastal.

QUINN DALTON is the author of the novel *High Strung* (2003) and short story collection *Bullet-Proof Girl* (2004). Over the years, she has sold cameras, ladies shoes, water filters, antiques, her wedding dress, and an old van. She's worked as a waiter, bartender, fund-raiser, trainer, freelance writer, and spin doctor, all of which continue to be a good source of material.

MEGHAN DAUM is the author of the essay collection *My Misspent Youth* (2001) and the novel *The Quality of Life Report* (2003). Her essays and articles have appeared in *The New Yorker, Harper's,* and *Vogue,* among other publications. She lives in Los Angeles with her dog, Rex, who is currently writing an essay on the gender politics of the dog community, called "Why Is That Bitch Ignoring Me?"

MELISSA DE LA CRUZ is the author of the novels *Cat's Meow* (2001) and *The Au Pairs* (2004). She coauthored the tongue-in-cheek nonfiction books *How to Become Famous in Two Weeks or Less* (2003) and *The Fashionista Files: Adventures in Four-Inch Heels and Faux Pas* (2004). She writes regularly for *Marie Claire, Harper's Bazaar, Lifetime, Gotham,* and *Hamptons* magazines and has contributed to *The New York Times, Glamour, Allure, Nerve,* and *McSweeney's.* Her work has been translated into many languages. She lives in Los Angeles with her husband, Michael Johnston.

SUSAN DOMINUS is a contributing writer at *The New York Times Magazine* and *Glamour,* which both pay her to do her favorite things: ask interesting people a lot of nosy questions, then opine loudly on the subject of what she's just heard.

EM AND LO (Emma Taylor and Lorelei Sharkey), the Emily Posts of the modern bedroom, coauthored *The Big Bang: Nerve's Guide to the New Sexual Universe* (2003) and *Nerve's Guide to Sex Etiquette* (2004). They write a monthly sex advice column for *Men's Journal* magazine and have contributed to numerous publications, including *Glamour* and *The Guardian* (UK). After four years as *Nerve's* resident advice gurus and "astrologists," they can now be found dishing about all things love-, sex-, and star-related on their own website, EmandLo.com. They both live in New York City, where they spend far too much time together.

LISA GABRIELE is a television producer, director, and cinematographer. Her writing has appeared in *The New York Times Magazine*, *The Washington Post*, *Nerve*, and *Vice*. Her first novel was *Tempting Faith DiNapoli* (2003). She has lived in Washington, D.C.; Whistler, British Columbia; New York City; Dawson City; Buenos Aires; and Toronto, where she is currently at work on her second novel.

DAISY GARNETT is a freelance writer living in London. Her work has appeared in *Vogue, Talk, New York* magazine, *The New York Times, The Guardian*, and the *Telegraph*.

MIKKI HALPIN is a freelance writer in New York City. She would like everyone to know that the events in the story took place several years ago and she is *way over* her ex now. Completely.

LYNN HARRIS is a journalist, author, comedian, and commentator on issues of gender, relationships, and pop culture. She is the cocreator of the superhero Breakup Girl (BreakupGirl.net), whose award-winning advice and adventures have appeared online, on TV, on stage, and in several books, including *Breakup Girl to the Rescue! A Superhero's Guide to Love, and Lack Thereof* (2000). Her novel, *Miss Media*, was published in 2004. Lynn, her articles, and observations have appeared in *The New York Times, Glamour*, the *New York Observer, Slate, Salon, New York, Entertainment Weekly, GQ*, and *Us Weekly*, as well as on numerous television and radio shows. Having (finally) met her husband through people she met at her fiftieth wedding, she feels that she is a portrait of hope.

PAM HOUSTON is the author of the short story collections *Cowboys Are My Weakness* (1992) and *Waltzing the Cat* (1999), and the novel *Sight Hound* (2005). Her stories have appeared in *Mirabella, Mademoiselle*, the *Mississippi Review*, and *Best American Short Stories*. Her nonfiction has appeared in *The New York Times, Vogue*, and *Nerve*.

AMY KEYISHIAN is a freelance magazine writer in New York, appearing in *Glamour, Maxim, Self*, and *Health*. She's also a contributing editor at the British edition of *Cosmopolitan*. When she can't sell a story, she writes romance novels for teens and hates it.

ERIKA KROUSE has published fiction in the *Atlantic Monthly, Story, Ploughshares, Shenandoah, Glamour*, and the Summer Fiction issue of *The New Yorker*. She is currently living in Boulder and working on a novel. Her collection of short stories, *Come Up and See Me Sometime* (2001), is the winner of the Paterson Fiction Award.

MERRILL MARKOE was a regular contributor to *Not Necessarily the News* and wrote and performed in several comedy specials for HBO throughout the eighties. She won Writers Guild and Ace awards for her participation with *NNTN*, as well as several Emmys for her writing for *Late Night with David Letterman*. Her books include *What the Dogs Have Taught Me and Other Amazing Things I've Learned* (1992), *How to Be Hap-Hap-Happy Like Me* (1994), *Merrill Markoe's Guide to Love* (1996), *It's My F—-ing Birthday* (2002), and *The Psycho Ex Game* (2004) with Andy Prieboy.

RACHEL MATTSON's essays have appeared in the *Village Voice*, *Nerve*, and on WNYC, among other places, and she is currently the historian-in-residence for a school district in the Bronx. Single and queer, she does, predictably, live in Brooklyn and have a cat. But she does not, under any circumstances, play softball. She is a huge fan of the Colombian indy rock group Aterciopelados.

ELIZA MINOT is the author of the novel *The Tiny One* (2000). Her work has appeared in the magazines *Real Simple, Allure, The New York Times Sunday Magazine*, and *Travel and Leisure Family*. Her second novel, *The Brambles*, is forthcoming. She lives in New Jersey with her husband and small children.

THISBE NISSEN is the author of a story collection, a cookbook-type-thing, and two novels, *The Good People of New York* (2002) and *Osprey Island* (2004). Thisbe loves her cats (Maisie and Fernanda), where she lives (Iowa), amateur musical theater (especially when they do Sondheim), name-your-baby books that actually have her name in them (Thisbe), beets (marinated in balsamic vinegar), tomatoes (and the smell of tomato plants), old Billy Joel (i.e., "All For Leyna"), and driving absurdly long distances while listening to Books on Tape (especially when Michael Prichard reads Don DeLillo). She kind of wishes she were a poet.

LAURIE NOTARO lives in Phoenix, where she eats inordinate amounts of Mexican food and sweats profusely. She is the author of *The Idiot Girls' Action-Adventure Club* (2002) and *Autobiography of a Fat Bride* (2003). Now married, she has not shaved for several years, except for the occasional job interview. She is usually unemployed.

ELISSA SCHAPPELL is the author of the novel *Use Me* (2001), which was a *New York Times* notable book, a *Los Angeles Times* best book of the year, a Border's Discover New Voices selection, and a runner up for the PEN/Hemingway award. She is also the Hot Type columnist for *Vanity Fair*, a founding editor of *Tin House* magazine, where she is now editor-at-large, and a former senior editor at *The Paris Review*. Her essays have appeared in *The Bitch in the House, Dog Culture,* and *Child of Mine.* Her short stories have been anthologized in or are forthcoming in *The KGB Bar Reader, Lit Riffs,* and *Night,* and they have also appeared in *BOMB, Witness, FAT, Interview, Literal Latte,* and *Nerve.* Her nonfiction and essays have also appeared in *The Paris Review, SPIN, Vogue, GQ, Glamour, Mademoiselle, The New York Times Book Review, SPY, BOOKFORUM, Harper's Bazaar, Salon,* and many more.

AMY SOHN is the author of the novels *Run Catch Kiss* (2001) and *My Old Man* (2004) and writes the "Naked City" column for *New York* magazine. She is also the author of *The New York Times* bestseller *Sex and the City: Kiss and Tell* (2002), the official companion guide to the hit HBO show.

JENNIFER WEINER grew up in Connecticut, studied English at Princeton, and spent ten years as a newspaper reporter in Pennsylvania and Kentucky before she published her first novel, *Good in Bed* (2001). Her other novels are *In Her Shoes* (2002) and *Little Earthquakes* (2004). She lives in Philadelphia with her husband and her daughter, who will not be allowed to read this essay, ever.

LIZ WELCH is a freelance writer whose work has appeared in *The New York Times Magazine, Vogue, Glamour, Cosmopolitan, Harper's Bazaar, Elle,* and many others.

HEATHER WHITE lives in Brooklyn in an illegal loft above a kosher juice drink factory. The squirrel-infested building is nestled between a freeway, two empty lots, and housing projects, so she rarely leaves her home and has ample time to reflect on her past sexual adventures. She recently married her brilliant artist husband and has an Italian greyhound that looks great in a sweater. This will be Heather's first published work since the seventh grade.

PRECIOUS WILLIAMS is the granddaughter of a Nigerian prince but grew up in England, where she worked as a fashion assistant, model, tabloid reporter, and celebrity interviewer before, and after, studying English literature at Oxford. Now a contributing editor at *Elle*, UK, and living in New York, Precious is working on her memoirs and a collection of short stories.

acknowledgments

Many thanks to my agent, Jenny Bent, whose idea it was to create a "*Sex and the Single Girl* for the new millennium," and who placed this book in the loving hands of Greer Hendricks and Suzanne O'Neill at Washington Square Press. And of course, to the twenty-nine writers who offered up their amazing true stories, and their hearts, when I called asking for the dirt.